Dash Diet Cookbook for Beginners:

The Ultimate Guide to Heart Health and Weight

Loss with Delicious Low-Sodium Recipes

30-Day Meal Plan of Healthy Eating

By TED DOLTON

Table of Contents

Introduction

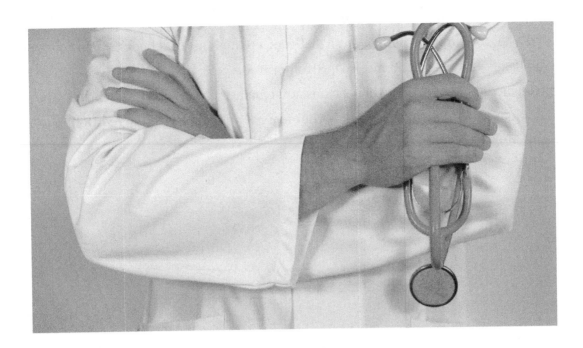

As the saying goes – **YOU ARE WHAT YOU EAT**.

What you consume daily tells a lot about your health and general well-being. Approximately 116 million adults in the United States have hypertension – but many are unaware of it.

High blood pressure, or hypertension, has serious health implications and is linked to higher stroke risks, heart attack, dementia, kidney failure, or premature death. So, your diet and lifestyle can significantly impact your health.

Struggling with hypertension can feel overwhelming and daunting – but the good news is, you can improve your blood pressure with diet. While medications are necessary to keep blood pressure in check, a dietary and lifestyle overhaul will significantly help manage your blood pressure and overall heart health.

The Dietary Approaches to Stop Hypertension was developed to help lower blood pressure without medication. It involves consuming fruits, vegetables, whole grains, low-fat dairy, fish, poultry, legumes, and vegetable oil while minimizing saturated fat, sugary beverages, and sweets.

The DASH Diet is proven effective and has been endorsed by the American Heart Association, The National Heart, Blood, and Lung Institute (NHLBI), and the Mayo Clinic to relieve hypertension, reduce the risk of heart diseases and improve overall heart health.

However, when taking the first steps to a new diet program, it can feel lofty to come up with meal ideas – what exactly should you eat? Needless to worry, with the DASH Diet Cookbook for Beginners 2023 by Ted Dolton, you can access a comprehensive list of Dash diet-friendly meals at your fingertips.

Written in an easy-to-follow and friendly style, this book shows you how to achieve your blood pressure mark while enjoying healthy, tasty, flavored meals. Plus, it cuts across all adults who suffer from hypertension, obesity, stress, and excessive alcohol. If you also experience difficulty following a healthy diet, this book is for you.

A Healthy diet is only as good as the food it provides in its plan. For this reason, Ted Dolton, with vast knowledge and over 20 years of experience as a dietician, created this cookbook to help you prepare fresh, nutritious, and healthy home-cooked meals DASH-approved.

Bursting with an incredible assortment of delicious homemade recipes, this guide will help you set yourself on a healthier and heart-smart future. So, allay your fears about hypertension; Ted Dolton is here to help you live a healthier lifestyle.

Part 1

Getting started with the Dash Diet

In this section, you'll understand everything you need to know about the DASH diet and its health benefits.

Chapter 1: Basics of Dash Diet and How to Use It

For some people, the concept of the DASH Diet sounds foreign. On the other hand, others may have heard it mentioned in the "It's time to change your lifestyle" speech. Regardless, diet plays a significant role in developing high blood pressure (hypertension).

A bad diet can lead to different health complications one does not envisage. One such complication is an abnormal blood pressure level. The higher your blood pressure level, the more at risk you are for other health problems like stroke, kidney failure, etc. Unfortunately, in a statistics report by the World Health Organization, an estimated 1.28 billion adults aged 30-79 years worldwide have hypertension.

Worse part; an estimated 46% of adults with hypertension are unaware that they have this condition. In the 1990s, the prevalence of hypertension led the National Institutes of Health (NIH) to propose funding to further research on the impact of specific dietary interventions on blood pressure. After teams of physicians conducted detailed research, nurses, nutritionists, statisticians, and research coordinators developed the DASH diet.

When you are diagnosed with hypertension, lifestyle modification, weight loss, and healthy eating are usually recommended by doctors to help curb it and reduce your body's susceptibility to a range of heart-related diseases.

What is a DASH Diet?

Dietary Approaches to Stop Hypertension is an adaptable, balanced, healthy-eating plan created to help treat or prevent high blood pressure (hypertension), diabetes, and heart-related diseases. While it is not specifically a weight loss diet, it can help you maintain a healthy weight.

The American Heart Association promotes this eating plan to stop or prevent high blood pressure, also known as hypertension. When the DASH Diet was developed, it originally featured a staple of starchy foods and grains. However, it was eventually modified into the form that we have today.

This diet relies on high-fiber foods, fresh fruits and vegetables, low-fat dairy, and healthy proteins such as seeds, beans, and nuts. Healthy eating starts with healthy food choices, and NO, you don't have to be a chef to create nutritious heart-healthy meals for you and your family.

Your healthy eating plan is about making smart choices to keep your health mark in check. To this end, the DASH diet focuses on eating:

- nutritious, fruit- and vegetable-based meals
- whole grains, non-tropical vegetable oils

- healthy sources of protein such as legumes and nuts; fish and seafood; low-fat or non-fat dairy; and unprocessed and lean meat
- Foods with minimal processing and low-sugars
- Low or no-salt foods
- Moderate or no alcohol intake.

Unfortunately, the availability of healthy food sources sometimes discourages people from following diet programs. But thankfully, DASH diet cookbooks like this are created to help streamline your choices and make meal planning easy.

How to Use the DASH Diet

To use the DASH diet for effective results, you will:

- Increase your intake of fruits, vegetables, and low-fat dairy products
- Limit saturated fats, cholesterol, and trans fats in your diet
- Consume more whole grains, poultry, fish, and nuts
- Ensure that your diet is rich in potassium, calcium, magnesium, fiber, and protein
- Be careful not to consume too much sodium, sweets, sugary drinks, red meat, and alcohol.

Benefits of the DASH Diet

With an overwhelming number of diet programs, knowing what works best for your body and lifestyle can take time and effort. But that is not the case with the DASH diet. This eating plan generally works for everyone, even if their health goals are slightly different.

The benefit of the DASH Diet is that those who follow it precisely begin to notice a decrease in their blood pressure and overall weight. Another perk of choosing the DASH Diet is the versatility that it offers to those who make it part of their daily routines.

For example, if you want a simple decrease in your sodium intake, you can choose the standard level of consumption of 2,300 milligrams. For those who want to eliminate a significant amount of sodium from their daily intake, their consumption is lowered to 1,500 milligrams daily.

Depending on your healthy eating goals, you can tailor your meals and level of consumption to suit your needs and preference. Additionally, thanks to the diet's high fruit and vegetable content, you can lower cholesterol and decrease the risk of cancer, diabetes, metabolic syndrome, and heart disease.

Finally, unlike other diets, the DASH diet is easy to adapt and stick to long term. It doesn't require special food or eliminate any food group. Plus, it is affordable, and the meals are delicious.

Chapter 2: Dash Diet & Hypertension

Hypertension is the force exerted by circulating blood against the walls of your arteries. The arteries carry blood from the heart to other parts of your body, and it's normal for the pressure to rise and decline throughout the day's activities.

Blood pressure is written as two numbers. The first number represents the pressure in blood vessels when your heart contracts or beats. The second one represents the pressure in the vessels when your heart rests between beats. An average blood pressure level measures less than 120/80mm HG.

Hypertension is a condition when the blood pressure is higher than average. Of course, the number changes based on your daily activities, but if it remains consistently above average, it may result in the diagnosis of high blood pressure or hypertension. People with a blood pressure of 140/90 mmHg or higher are considered to have high blood pressure.

Unfortunately, the higher your blood pressure, the greater the risk of other health conditions like stroke, heart disease, heart attack, etc. High blood pressure makes the heart work too hard, contributing to the hardening of the arteries. According to the World Health Organization, hypertension is a significant cause of premature deaths worldwide.

High blood pressure (hypertension) usually develops over time and can occur due to several risk factors and unhealthy lifestyle choices. Fortunately, you can control most of these risk factors:

- Excessive salt consumption
- Unhealthy eating,
- Consuming a diet high in saturated fats
- Physical Inactivity,
- Alcohol & tobacco consumption.
- Diabetes
- Obesity

Your chances of developing heart disease multiply greatly if you have multiple risk factors. Unfortunately, hypertension has no warning signs or symptoms, and many people are unaware they have it. Regularly measuring your blood pressure is the only way to manage this condition.

Preventing Hypertension

As already mentioned, you can take action to control these risk factors. Besides medications, people with hypertension can lower their blood pressure and maintain a healthy range by making positive lifestyle changes. Engaging in physical activities, eating a healthy diet, avoiding alcohol and smoking, or managing stress can help keep your blood pressure in check.

As mentioned in Chapter 1, choosing healthy meals and snacks enables you to avoid high pressure and its complications. One proven and effective way to achieve this is by incorporating the DASH Diet. Switching to this eating plan doesn't mean sacrificing good food.

Instead, you fill up fresh fruits, vegetables, and delicious meals rich in potassium, calcium, magnesium, protein, etc.

When it comes to your cardiovascular health, blood pressure, and diet, salt plays a huge role. For instance, salt makes your body hold onto water. When you consume too much, the extra water in your blood increases blood pressure.

In the same vein, saturated fat can boost bad cholesterol, also linked to hypertension. Eating fatty foods can also increase visceral fat in your body which is dangerous and can raise blood pressure by physically compressing the kidneys.

Scientific studies have shown that reducing salt intake can lead to a reduction in hypertension. So, the DASH diet also advocates lower salt intake.

This eating plan is safe, nutritious, easy to follow, and effective for short and long-term weight loss. Suffice it to say that the DASH diet is not a quick fix but a lifetime solution.

Dash diet has a proven record of helping people lower their blood pressure and keep other illnesses at bay. Compared to a standard diet, adults following this diet without altering sodium intake can lower their blood pressure within weeks.

Those who reduced their sodium intake from 3,450 mg to 2,300 mg or less per day have even more significant reductions in blood pressure. People with high blood pressure who adopt a low-sodium DASH diet see the most remarkable improvements in their health.

If you are diagnosed with hypertension, you and your healthcare provider should work together to curb it. You need to concur on your blood pressure goal and devise a plan and timetable for achieving it. If you are advised to follow a healthy meal, don't despair. You won't be eating salads daily for lunch, which is guaranteed.

By following through with the meal plans and recipes in the coming chapters, you can control high blood pressure and live a healthier life. While you read them, think to yourself, **"I Can Do It!"**

Chapter 3: Effect of Dash Diet on Weight Management

Losing weight is likely recommended if you already have high blood pressure. Too much weight strains your heart, increasing the risk of developing hypertension and other heart diseases.

Reaching and maintaining a healthy weight can be quite challenging for most people. Your weight loss attempts may have failed in the past. Be assured you are not alone in this fight. Thankfully, the DASH diet is also effective for weight management beyond reducing blood pressure and cholesterol levels.

The Keys to Healthy Weight Loss

Achieving your weight loss goals isn't just about a diet or program. Instead, it's about living a healthy lifestyle with a healthy eating pattern, regular exercise, and stress management. When trying to lose weight, it's normal for you to expect a positive result very quickly. But, those who gradually shed weight are more likely to keep it off and maintain it long-term.

The key to healthy weight management is to be on a calorie deficit. It begins with these simple yet essential steps:

- Follow an overall healthy diet pattern
- Watch what you eat
- Choose healthy and nutritious foods
- Eat lots of fruits, vegetables, and whole grains
- Consume more poultry, fish, and nuts, and reduce the consumption of red meat
- Reduce or eliminate saturated and trans fats, added sugars, and sodium from your diet
- Choose fat-free and low-fat dairy products
- Cut out beverages and foods high in calories with little to no nutritional benefits
- Prepare your meals with little or no salt
- Be physically active.

DASH Diet and Weight Management

The DASH eating plan was not created to promote weight loss but to help treat hypertension. However, you can seamlessly achieve your weight loss goals because it is rich in antioxidants and low-calorie foods like fruits, vegetables, whole grains, and low-fat dairy products.

A higher fruit and vegetable intake helps you ingest large antioxidants that further aid in combatting oxidative stress, lower blood pressure, also lowering your risk of heart disease. Unlike other diets such as Keto, Dukan, and Whole30, which are restrictive regarding the food they allow, the DASH diet is flexible and sustainable. You can easily prepare them at home whether or not you are busily employed.

The DASH diet is intended to be integrated into your lifestyle, emphasizing eating less processed food, cutting back on refined carbohydrates, alcohol reduction, physical activity, stress reduction, no smoking, and getting quality sleep. By combining this eating plan with calorie cutting, you healthily lose weight. With this DASH Diet cookbook, you can easily modify the daily portions from all the different food groups into practical meals. From years of practice and experience, I have helped beginners create personalized meal plans, considering their adjustments for food allergies and offering valuable tips for following the plan.

You can even discover new meals that will quickly become your favorites. So, if your DASH diet goal is weight management, this eating plan won't shed off the excess pounds quickly. But when you identify your calorie level and stick with it consistently, you can manage your weight while improving your health. Finally, ignore your subconscious mind discouraging you from starting this journey - DASH diet recipes are perfect for weight loss management. Once you reach your healthy weight goal, continue to balance your amount of calorie intake with the amount of energy you burn daily to maintain your weight. The fiber and protein will keep you satiated, while the calorie content will keep you energized.

Chapter 4: Advantages of Following Dash Diet

As you've learned in the previous chapters, there are great benefits attached to adopting DASH dieting. In addition to promoting your blood pressure control, the DASH diet can help you fight diabetes and boost your energy level. Yes, it can improve your insulin resistance, hyperlipidemia, and obesity (I'll get into this shortly.)

DASH Diet and Diabetes Nutrition

Diabetes and hypertension are somewhat sisters- they go hand-in-hand. More than half of people diagnosed with diabetes also have high blood pressure. Nutritional therapy promotes healthy eating patterns to help with the management of diabetes. However, making food choices that keep your blood sugar level within range can be overwhelming.

Positive eating habits can lead to excellent outcomes. It's no wonder diabetes educators often recommend the DASH diet to their patients with diabetes. It focuses on fruits, vegetables, low-fat dairy, lean meat, whole grains, beans, and nuts. The diet also limits sodium, red meat, sugary foods, and drinks that harm one's health.

Also, the DASH diet affects weight loss, insulin sensitivity, and glycemic control. With this, you can lower the risk of Type 2 diabetes; if you already have it, you can best maintain your health. Again, it is nutritious, balanced, practical, and sustainable in the long haul. It can suit your needs, circumstances, and lifestyle.

Valid Reasons Why You Should Follow Dash Diet

I must emphasize the importance and benefits of the DASH diet on your heart health and general well-being.

- **It Minimizes the Risk of Heart Disease**

The DASH diet has gained wide recognition for its ability to lower blood pressure and minimize the risk of heart disease. This diet is also a good choice for those with a family history of heart problems. Its nutritional regimen will help you live a healthy life without unnecessary ailments while enjoying tasty meals.

- **It is Affordable**

You can follow the DASH diet long-term because it is budget-friendly. You can find foods for this diet at your typical grocery store. It doesn't require any expensive or exotic.

- **It is Family Friendly**

You and your family can enjoy healthy, delicious meals with little or no modifications. The food options contained in this cookbook are balanced enough for all ages. You can easily modify meals for vegans or those looking to follow the halal diet.

- **It Lowers Hyperlipidemia**

Hyperlipidemia is when your blood contains too many lipids or fats, such as cholesterol and triglycerides. Thankfully, high cholesterol can be lowered, thus reducing the risks of stroke or other heart diseases. With the DASH diet, you reduce your intake of saturated and trans fat. You focus more on healthy alternatives like fruits, vegetables, and non-tropical oils.

- **It is Packed With Healthy Nutrients**

The DASH diet gives you all the essential nutrients your body needs. You get filled with nutritious meals from fruits, vegetables, nuts, whole grains, poultry, etc.

- **It is Flexible**

The DASH diet is easy to follow. While giving up your sugary, fatty comfort food may be challenging, the DASH diet does not restrict the entire food group. With so many DASH-friendly recipes, you should be able to use them long-term. If you wish for more flexibility, you can tweak your meals and still reap the heart health benefits of DASH.

- **It Aids in Weight Loss**

Are your DASH diet goals for weight loss? Then this eating plan is a great place to start. You can lose weight and maintain it, as explained in Chapter 3.

- **It is not Boring but Delicious**.

Last, ignore the nay-sayers- a healthy diet doesn't have to be boring. You can enjoy diverse foods and flavors without missing out on unhealthy food options. For example, if you love salty food, you may need help with accepting low-sodium meals. However, your taste buds will adjust with time and leap for more low-salt diets.

Regardless of what benefits you are going for, the DASH diet can be adapted based on your cultural or food preferences.

Chapter 5: Ten (10) Key Habits to Feel Healthier With the Dash Diet

There are fundamental lifestyle changes you can inculcate into your daily to get the most out of the diet and control your blood pressure for life. Let's list some of them.

- **Be Physically Active**

Get your body moving. A sedentary lifestyle is bad for your physical health and well-being. And no- you don't have to hit the gym to be physically active. Brisk walking, running, swimming, bicycling, and even doing some yard work will keep your heart pumping and your body happy.

Being physically active helps to relieve stress, improves your mood, helps you sleep better, and reduces your risk of diseases. So move more, sit less!

- **Maintain a Healthy Weight**

Stress, depression, emotional eating, or cravings can make maintaining a healthy weight difficult. Regardless, you need to maintain a healthy weight o help prevent and control hypertension and other ailments.

So, instead of unhealthy meals, fill your belly with colorful fruits and vegetables and ensure you don't get too hungry between meals. Finally, if emotional eating is a problem, address it head-on with your doctor or therapist.

- **Limit Alcohol Intake**

Drinking alcohol can raise your blood pressure to unhealthy levels. Alcohol contains calories that can cause weight gain. So, whether or not you are hypertensive, drinking frequently is discouraged.

- **Get Plenty of Quality Sleep**

Sleep is as crucial for your health as exercise and diet. Unfortunately, many factors can interfere with a night of good sleep- from work, illness, stress, or family responsibilities. Insufficient sleep increases the risk of many diseases like hypertension, heart disease, stroke, obesity, and dementia.

While you may not be able to control these factors, you can adopt habits to encourage quality sleep. For example, stick to a sleep schedule, create a restful environment, avoid large meals before bedtime, manage your worries, etc.

- **Manage Stress**

We all feel stress at every point in our lives. But stress that lasts for weeks can affect your physical and mental health. So, you must learn to identify and manage your stressors for optimal health.

Some people fall back on unhealthy patterns like emotional eating, drinking, or smoking when stressed. While these patterns may comfort you initially, they can harm you in the long run. So start with the basics- set your priorities, get organized, delegate tasks where necessary, exercise, and try meditating.

- **Quit Smoking**

Similar to alcohol, smoking is bad for your health. Vaping and tobacco use lower your HDL (good) cholesterol, meaning there is less good cholesterol to remove bad cholesterol from your arteries. Beyond hurting your body, smoking can increase anxiety, depression, irritability, impatience, hostility, difficulty concentrating, restlessness, decreased heart rate, or weight gain. Combining the DASH diet with zero tobacco use sets you on a path to a healthy lifestyle.

- **Drink Plenty of Fluids**

Choose water instead of soda or juice. You need about 2 liters (8 cups) of fluid daily to stay hydrated and healthy. Water is always the best choice, but other beverages can work too. Unsweetened tea or coffee without sugar can help. If you dislike the flavor of water, add your preferred fruits and chug it down.

- **Shop Smart**

When you visit the grocery store, be smart about your shopping. Check for food labels. Choose items that are low in sodium as well as unhealthy fats. In Part Two of this book, I list items to include in your DASH grocery list.

- **Limit Eating Out**

While dining out saves you time to meal prep and cook, finding meals that fit your diet can be challenging. The DASH diet does not restrict eating out; however, there are tips you ensure you stay on track. So if you must eat out, choose healthy options and avoid choosing menus that conflict with your goals.

- **Speak With Your Doctor**

Your doctor or a registered nutritionist should be your friend for healthy living. If you have any questions or concerns about the DASH diet or any diet plan, they should help you address same.

Changing many habits at once can be overwhelming when starting a new healthy lifestyle. So start one at a time, and remember to celebrate your success (in a healthy way) once you start seeing positive changes.

Part 2

Dash Grocery List

In this section, you'll find what food products I recommend under the DASH diet and tips for food shopping.

Chapter 6: Checking Out Your Shopping List

Shopping on the DASH diet is relatively easy. Everything you need is accessible at your local grocery store. It doesn't require any special food or expensive budgets that can put you off. However, you should learn to read nutrition labels on items to check for excessive fat content or high sodium levels. If you are still trying to decide what to buy when shopping, I have compiled this comprehensive list to guide you as you begin your DASH diet journey.

Fresh Vegetables

Artichokes

Asparagus

Beets

Bell peppers

Broccoli

Brussels sprouts

Cabbage

Carrots

Cauliflower

Celery

Corn

Cucumbers

Eggplant

Green beans

Mushrooms

Leafy greens: collards, kale, or turnip greens

Lettuce or salad greens

Onions

Peas: green peas, snap peas, or snow peas

Potatoes or sweet potatoes

Radishes

Root vegetables

Spinach

Summer squash: zucchini, yellow, crookneck

Sprouts

Tomatoes Winter squash: acorn, butternut, pumpkin, or spaghetti squash

Fresh Fruits

Apples

Apricots

Bananas

Berries: strawberries, blueberries, raspberries, or blackberries

Cherries Citrus: grapefruit, oranges, or tangerines

Dates

Grapes

Kiwi fruit

Lemons or limes

Watermelon

Nectarines or peaches

Papaya

Pears

Pineapple

Plums

Prunes

Raisins

Dairy

Buttermilk (low-fat)

Cheese (hard): reduced-fat cheddar, Monterey jack, parmesan

Cheese (soft): blue, goat cheese , feta

Cottage cheese (low-fat)

Milk (fat-free or low-fat)

Flavored milk (fat-free or low-fat)

Kefir Margarine (trans-fat-free)

Mozzarella (part-skim)

Sour cream (low-fat)

Yogurt (fat-free or low-fat)

Meat, Poultry, and Sea Food

Beef: flank, round, or sirloin

Beef, turkey, chicken (ground, lean)

Chicken or turkey (skinless)

Eggs

Lamb

Pork tenderloin

Fish fillets (plain)

Sliced deli meat

Salmon

Shrimp

Tempeh

Tofu

Bread and Grains

Bagels

Whole Wheat Bread

Barley

English muffins

Pizza crust

Tortillas (corn or whole-wheat)

Brown rice

Bulgur

Couscous (whole wheat)

Kasha (buckwheat)

Oats (old-fashioned)

Pasta (whole wheat)

Quinoa

Millet, Amaranth Spelt

Triticale

Kamut

Cereal Wild rice

Nuts and Seeds

Almonds

Cashews

Hazelnuts

Nut butter (peanut, almond, etc.)

Peanuts

Pecans

Pumpkin seeds or sunflower

Soy nuts

Walnuts

Beverages

100 % Fruit juice

Diet soda

Herbal tea

Sparkling water

Chapter 7: What To Eat and What To Avoid With the Dash Diet

As you've learned in the previous chapters, the DASH diet encourages you to eat foods rich in potassium, calcium, and magnesium. Again, plenty of fruits and vegetables, fish, poultry, lean meats, beans, lentils, nuts, whole grains, and low-fat dairy are your go-to sources for fueling your hunger and reducing blood pressure.

Let me show you if you are still wondering what you can eat.

What Should I Eat?

The DASH diet is set to provide daily and weekly nutritional goals. The DASH diet does not require you to count calories. Instead, what you eat daily is built around each DASH food group's recommended number of servings.

Your recommended calorie target determines the servings allowed for various food groups. To determine your DASH diet calorie goals, you must consider your age, gender, activity level, and medical conditions. The recommended servings for each food group are based on 2,000 calories a day. Serving sizes can be increased or decreased for other calorie levels. You can make gradual changes along the way.

For example, limit yourself to 2,300 milligrams of sodium per day (about one teaspoon). When your body has adjusted to the diet, cut back to 1,500 milligrams of sodium daily (about 2/3 teaspoons). Daily sodium levels are either 2,300 milligrams or, by making the suggested changes, 1,500 milligrams.

Let me break down daily servings based on 2000 calories per day.

- **Grains:** 7 to 8 servings a day. With at least three whole-grain food consumed each day. Some instances include a slice of whole-wheat bread, 1 ounce of dry whole-grain cereal, or 1/2 of cooked cereal, rice, or pasta.

- **Fruits:** 4 to 5 servings a day. Such as one portion is one medium fruit, 1/2 cup fresh or frozen fruit, or 1/2 cup fruit juice.

- **Vegetables:** 4 to 5 servings a day. For example, 1 cup leafy green vegetable, 1/2 cup cut-up raw or cooked vegetables.

- **Poultry, lean meats, and fish**: 6 one-ounce servings or fewer a day. For example, one ounce of cooked lean meat, skinless poultry, fish, 1 egg, and 2 egg whites.

- **Nuts and legumes:** 4 to 5 servings a week. Such as 1/3 cup nuts, 2 tablespoons peanut butter or seeds, and 1/2 cup cooked legumes (dried beans or peas).

- **Low-fat dairy products:** 2 or 3 servings a day. Such as 1 cup serving of low-fat or fat-free milk/yogurt or 1 1/2 ounces of low-fat or fat-free cheese.

- **Fats and oils:** 2 or 3 servings a day. For example, 1 teaspoon soft margarine, 1 teaspoon vegetable oil or mayonnaise, or 2 tablespoons low-fat salad dressing.

- **Sweets and added sugars:** 4 servings or fewer a week. One serving is 1 tablespoon of sugar, 1 tablespoon of jelly or jam, or 1 cup of lemonade.

Chapter 9: Frequently Asked Questions (FAQ) Section

While the DASH diet is relatively straightforward, people still ask a few questions about it. Here are some answers to your frequently asked questions on the DASH diet.

What Does the DASH diet stand for?

DASH diet stands for (Dietary Approaches to Stop Hypertension). It is a balanced diet rich in potassium and reduced in sodium. It has been tested and proven to prevent or lower the risk of hypertension (high blood pressure).

How many versions of the DASH diet are available?

There are two types of the DASH diet- the standard DASH diet and the Low Sodium DASH diet. The Standard DASH diet suggests people eat no more than 2,300 milligrams (mg) of salt daily, while the Low Sodium DASH diet limits sodium intake to 1,500 milligrams (mg) daily. Both versions aim to reduce sodium consumption.

What types of food are allowed in the DASH diet?

The DASH diet is a heart-healthy plan that can help you control the risk of heart disease through healthy foods. The plan emphasizes eating fresh fruits and vegetables, low-fat dairy products, whole-grains, lean meat, seafood, poultry, fish, nuts, and seeds.

Can a DASH diet help with weight loss?

The DASH diet is rich in lower-calorie foods like fruits and vegetables to support your weight loss goals. However, it's advised not to rely on this eating plan alone to shed unwanted pounds, as it is primarily designed to improve heart health.

I am allergic to dairy. Can I still follow the DASH diet?

Short answer- "Absolutely." The DASH diet is highly accommodating to dietary restrictions. Those who are lactose intolerant can participate and actively follow the DASH diet. However, you may need to modify the diet to include lactose-free alternatives to dairy. But ensure that the milk substitutes have comparable calcium and vitamin D levels as the original foods.

Is the DASH diet suitable for everyone?

No! Firstly, the DASH diet was developed following research that those who follow a diet high in plant-based foods are less likely to develop high blood pressure. So it is effective and recommended for only those who want to prevent or treat hypertension, also known as high blood pressure.

However, healthy individuals don't need it and may benefit more from other dietary approaches tailored to their nutritional needs.

Do I need to exercise while on a DASH diet?

The DASH diet is not just a diet plan but a lifestyle change. For it to be successful, there are other lifestyle changes you should make to prevent hypertension and boost your health. Combining the DASH diet with regular physical activities will help bring some additional health benefits and help you stay fit.

Are there other potential benefits of the DASH diet plan?

The DASH diet is effective in preventing or reducing the chances of heart disease, high blood pressure, metabolic syndrome, stroke, diabetes, kidney failure, and cancer, and it also improves your heart health. It can also help you lose and maintain weight if needed. Finally, stick with the DASH diet and enjoy health benefits.

Part 4

Dash Diet Recipes

Here, you will find fun, easy, and delicious DASH-friendly recipes. Remember to use fresh, organic, and unprocessed ingredients whenever possible as you read through. Enjoy!

DASH Diet Breakfast Recipes

Breakfast is the most important meal of the day. Eating a meal in the morning jump-starts your metabolism for the day. Here are healthy, fresh, and quick breakfast recipes to start your DASH-eating way.

Veggie Tuna Sandwich

Preparation Time: 10 min

Cooking Time: 10 min | Servings: 4

Ingredients

8 large green lettuce or red leaf lettuce

8 slices of whole-grain bread

2 (6-ounce) cans of tuna, drained

½ cup of mayonnaise for spreading on the bread

½ tsp each of salt and pepper to taste

⅛ cup of green onion finely diced

½ cup of celery finely diced

Preparation

1. Combine the tuna, mayonnaise, green onion, and celery in a medium or large bowl. Add ½ teaspoon of salt and black pepper to taste.
2. Divide the tuna mixture between four pieces of bread.
3. Layer the two lettuce leaves on the other four slices of bread.
4. Assemble the two sides of each sandwich.
5. Slice and serve your sandwich to enjoy.

Nutritional value

Calories: 277kcal | Carbohydrates: 3g | Protein: 18g | Fat: 22g | Saturated Fat: 3g | Cholesterol: 42mg | Sodium: 490mg | Potassium: 256mg | Dietary Fiber: 1g | Sugar: 1g| Calcium: 34mg |

Applesauce and Baked Oatmeal Bars

Preparation Time: 10 min

Cooking Time: 25 min | Servings: 6

Ingredients

1 egg

½ cup of applesauce sweetened

1 ½ cups of non-fat or 1% milk

1 tsp of vanilla

2 tbsps of oil

About 1 ½ cups of chopped apple

2 cups of rolled oats

1 tsp of baking powder

¼ tsp of salt

1 tsp of cinnamon

Toppings:

2 tbsps of chopped nuts

2 tbsps of brown sugar

Preparation

1. First of all, preheat the oven to a temperature of 375°F.
2. Prepare a baking pan of about 8 inches by 8 inches, lightly oil or spray the pan, and leave aside.
3. Combine the egg, applesauce, milk, vanilla, and oil in a bowl. Add the apple. Mix the rolled oats, baking powder, salt, and cinnamon separately. Add to the liquid ingredients and mix well. Pour the mixture into a baking dish and bake for 25-30 minutes until well browned.

4. Remove from the oven and sprinkle 2 tbsps of the brown sugar and nuts on the surface.

5. Return to the oven and broil for 3-4 minutes until the top is browned and the sugar bubbles.

6. Remove from the oven and cut into squares of your preference.

7. Serve warm to enjoy, and refrigerate leftovers for future use.

Nutritional value

Calories: 206kcal | Carbohydrates: 25g | Protein: 5g | Fat: 10g | Saturated Fat: 6g | Cholesterol: 53mg | Sodium: 448mg | Potassium: 126mg | Dietary Fiber: 2g | Sugar: 11g | Calcium: 87mg |

Morning Burrito

Preparation Time: 5 min
Cooking Time: 5 min | Servings: 4

Ingredients

½ cup of fat-free Cheddar cheese

4 whole wheat tortillas

¼ cup of chopped onion

¼ cup of low-fat milk

⅓ tsp of ground pepper

1 cup boiled black beans

2 whole eggs

4 egg whites

½ cup salsa

Preparation

1. Firstly, whisk eggs, egg whites, pepper, and milk in a microwave-friendly dish. Put the dish in the microwave and cook on high heat for 3 minutes. Remove the dish and stir the egg mixture evenly.

2. Place tortillas on a clean surface and add the egg mixture evenly. Add black beans, cheddar cheese, and chopped onions.

3. Transfer tortillas to a flat plate and microwave for 2 minutes.

4. Top the tortillas with salsa to enjoy.

Nutritional value

Calories: 291kcal | Carbohydrates: 38.5g | Protein: 20g | Fat: 7.6g | Sugar: 1.8g | Cholesterol: 95mg | Sodium: 570mg | Potassium: 345.5mg | Dietary Fiber: 7.5g

Vegan Sweet Potato Oats Waffles

Preparation Time: 3 min
Cooking Time: 3 min | Servings: 2 to 3

Ingredients

⅓ cup of cooked sweet potato (mashed) or sweet potato puree

1½ cups of oat flour

1 tsp of cinnamon

1 tsp of baking powder

A pinch of salt

1 chia or flax egg (1 tsp chia seeds or flax + 3 tsp warm water)

1 cup of plant milk

Olive oil

1 tsp maple syrup (optional)

Preparation

1. Take a cooked and peeled sweet potato and mash it. Combine it with non-dairy milk and vegan egg (chia seeds or flax combined with water), and set the batter aside while preheating the waffle iron.

2. Combine all dry ingredients (oat flour, cinnamon, and baking powder) in a large

bowl. *Simple grind oats in a blender until they are a fine flour consistency*.

3. Whisk together all wet ingredients in a small bowl, then fold them into dry.

4. Cook in a well-oiled waffle iron until you've reached your desired crispiness.

5. Serve warm with maple syrup or your desired toppings, and enjoy.

Nutritional value

Calories: 293kcal | Carbohydrates: 39g |Saturated fat: 1g| Protein: 10g | Fat: 11g | Sugar: 6g | Cholesterol: 0mg | Sodium: 162mg | Potassium: 345.5mg | Dietary Fiber: 5g |

Open-Faced Breakfast Sandwich

Preparation Time: 3 min
Cooking Time: 2 min | Servings: 1

Ingredient

½ cup spinach

1 slice of 100% whole wheat bread

2 tomato slices

1 ½ tsp olive oil

2 egg whites, beaten

Cracked black pepper, to taste

1 tsp brown mustard

1 thin slice of low-fat cheddar cheese

Preparation

1. First, preheat your toaster oven to 400°F. Get a small non-stick pan and heat on medium heat. Add oil to the hot pan, and add the egg whites when the oil sizzles. Scramble the eggs while cooking, add the spinach, and season to taste with pepper.

2. On your whole wheat bread, spread the mustard sparingly, add the tomato and scrambled eggs, and top with cheese. Heat in

the oven for about two minutes until the cheese melts. Serve to enjoy.

Nutritional value

Calories: 286kcal | Carbohydrates: 27g |Calcium: 15%| Protein: 20g |Total Fat: 12g |Sugar: 0.1g | Cholesterol: 6mg | Sodium: 515mg | Potassium: 344mg | Dietary Fiber: 4g | Saturated Fat: 3g |

Broccoli Omelet

Preparation Time: 5 min
Cooking Time: 7 min | Servings: 1

Ingredients:

2 egg whites

1 whole egg

2 tsp of extra virgin olive oil

½ cup of chopped broccoli

1 large clove of garlic, minced

⅛ tsp of chile pepper flakes

¼ cup low-fat feta cheese

Cracked black pepper

Preparation

1. Whisk the egg whites and egg in a small bowl. Heat a small non-stick pan on medium heat.

2. Add 1 tablespoon of the oil to the hot pan, and when the oil is hot, add the broccoli. Cook for 2 minutes before adding the garlic, chile pepper flakes, and black pepper to taste.

3. Cook for 2 minutes more; remove the broccoli mixture from the pan and place it in a separate bowl.

4. Turn the heat to low, add the tablespoon of olive oil, and add the whisked eggs when the oil is hot. Once they start to bubble and pull away from the sides, about 30 seconds, flip the omelet over and immediately scoop the

broccoli mixture and feta cheese on one half of the omelet.

5. Fold the omelet over, turn off the heat, and cover the pan with a cap for 2 minutes.

6. Serve immediately to enjoy.

Nutritional value

Calories: 493kcal | Carbohydrates: 6g |Calcium: 23g| Protein: 29g |Total Fat: 41g |Sugar: 0g | Cholesterol: 205mg | Sodium: 984mg | Potassium: 368mg | Dietary Fiber: 3g | Saturated Fat: 11g |

Veggie Frittata with Caramelized Onions

Preparation Time: 10 min

Cooking Time: 20 min | Servings: 6

Ingredients

Caramelized Onions:

1 tbsp extra virgin olive oil

1 small white onion, thinly sliced

¼ tsp brown sugar

⅛ tsp cracked black pepper

Frittata:

1 cup of thinly sliced cremini mushrooms

2-3 tsp of finely chopped fresh basil

2-3 tsp of extra virgin olive oil

1 ½ cups of chopped zucchini

1 clove garlic, minced

1 tsp of chopped fresh parsley or 1 tsp of dried parsley

2 cups of spinach

4 whole eggs

5 egg whites

½ cup of 1% milk

½ cup of shredded low-fat pepper jack cheese

⅛ tsp of sea salt

Cracked black pepper

Preparation

1. First, preheat the oven to 350°F.

2. To caramelize the onions, take a medium saucepan over medium heat. Add the oil, onion, sugar, and pepper. Sautée the onion and stir every few minutes to avoid burning. Continue for about 10 minutes until it is light brown and softened. Turn off the heat and cover the pan until ready to serve.

3. Start the frittata by heating a large pan over medium heat and then add the oil. Toss in the zucchini, and cook for about a minute. Add the garlic, and cook for 2 to 3 more minutes before adding the mushrooms, basil, and parsley.

4. Cook vegetables for another minute, sprinkle on salt and pepper. Mix, turn off the heat, and then add the spinach.

5. Whisk the eggs, egg whites, milk, shredded cheese, salt, and pepper in a bowl.

6. Spray a cake pan with olive oil spray. Pour in the sautéed ingredients and then the egg mixture. Place the pan into the oven, and cook for 20 to 25 minutes.

7. Once cooled, serve to enjoy.

Nutritional value

Calories: 197kcal | Carbohydrates: 6g |Calcium: 18g| Protein: 14g |Total Fat: 14g |Sugar: 2g | Cholesterol: 135mg | Sodium: 394mg | Potassium: 329mg | Dietary Fiber: 1g | Saturated Fat: 4g |

Mediterranean Scramble

Preparation Time: 10 min

Cooking Time: 10 min | Servings: 1

Ingredients

2 tablespoons of extra virgin olive oil

⅛ cup of chopped red onion

1 medium clove garlic, minced

¼ cup of sliced red bell pepper

¼ cup rinsed and drained, chopped canned artichoke hearts

1 whole egg

2 egg whites

⅛ tsp of dried oregano

⅛ tsp of cracked black pepper

⅛ cup of low-fat feta cheese

Preparation

1. Heat a small non-stick pan on medium heat. Add oil to the hot pan, and add the onion and garlic when it is hot. Cook for 1 minute before adding the bell pepper strips and artichoke hearts.

2. Sautée the vegetables for another 3 minutes until the onion is translucent and the bell pepper is softened.

3. Whisk the egg whites and egg in another small bowl and season with oregano and black pepper.

4. Next, pour the eggs in and mix them with a spatula. Cook for 3 - 4 minutes or until the eggs are no longer runny. Remove from heat, top with feta, and cover until the feta starts to melt. Serve to enjoy!

Nutritional value

Calories: 424kcal | Carbohydrates: 5g |Calcium: 11%| Protein: 21g |Total Fat: 37g |Sugar: 1g | Cholesterol: 195mg | Sodium: 572mg | Potassium: 179mg | Dietary Fiber: 1g | Saturated Fat: 8g | Magnesium: 2%|

Monkey Shake

Preparation Time: 5 min

Cooking Time: 5 min | Servings: 1

Ingredients

½ peeled orange (leave the pithy white part on or hand juice the orange)

1/2 papaya, peeled

1 banana

Juice orange with papaya.

Preparation

1. Place juice and banana in a blender and blend until smooth.

2. Garnish with the orange twist.

3. Pour into a tall glass and enjoy!

Nutritional value

Calories: 204kcal | Carbohydrates: 49g |Protein: 2g |Total Fat: 0g |Sugar: 29g | Cholesterol: 0mg | Sodium: 5mg |Dietary Fiber: 7g | Saturated Fat: 0g |

Onion and Asparagus Frittata

Preparation Time: 10 min

Cooking Time: 20 min | Servings: 2-3

Ingredients

1 tsp olive oil

6 large eggs

¼ cup plus 1 tbsp parmesan cheese, grated

1 medium onion, thinly sliced

2 tsp balsamic vinegar

2 cups (about 1 bunch) of asparagus, cut into 1-inch sections

3 green onions, sliced

¼ cup fresh basil, thinly sliced

½ tsp kosher salt

Fresh ground pepper to taste

Preparation

1. Preheat the broiler to a high temperature. Heat an oven-proof dish for a few minutes.
2. Pour the olive oil and heat well. Then toss the sliced onion and cook for about 5 minutes until soft and tender.
3. Next, pour the vinegar into the onion mixture.
4. Toss in the cut asparagus and water (about 2 tbsps), cover, and steam for about 5 minutes.
5. While that is on, place the eggs in a bowl and whisk well. Toss in ¼ cup of parmesan, ¼ tsp salt, and a dash of pepper.
6. Mix in the sliced green onions, sliced basil, and balanced salt to the asparagus mixture. Spoon the whisked egg mixture into the asparagus and mix well.
7. Use a spatula to bring the cooked egg to the surface. Leave for about 2-3 minutes for the ingredients to cook through.
8. Leave the pan under the broiler for 3-4 minutes, and add the cheese.
9. Allow the pan to be kept under the broiler for about 3 minutes until the mixture is slightly brown.
10. Take out from the broiler and add 1 tbsp of parmesan. Leave for 5 minutes and remove the frittata from the pan to a wooden cutting board.
11. Once cooled, cut into your desired portion and enjoy.

Nutritional value

Calories: 88.3kcal | Carbohydrates: 2.7g |Calcium: 11.2g| Protein: 14g |Total Fat: 5.3g |Sugar: 0.6g | Cholesterol: 69.3mg | Sodium: 203.2mg | Potassium: 149.1mg | Dietary Fiber: 0.7g | Saturated Fat: 2.9g | Magnesium: 2.8mg|

Banana Nutty Pancakes

Preparation Time: 5 min

Cooking Time: 5 min | Servings: 2

Ingredients

1 cup whole wheat flour

2 tbsp of baking powder

¼ tsp of salt

2 tsp of chopped walnuts

¼ tsp of cinnamon

1 large banana, mashed

1 cup 1% milk

3 large egg whites

2 tsp of oil

1 tsp of vanilla

Preparation

1. All the dry ingredients mix in a large bowl. Pour the milk into another bowl.
2. Next, separate the eggs and add the egg whites to the milk.
3. Mix in the vanilla, mashed banana, and oil and combine wet and dry ingredients, ensuring not to over-mix.
4. Heat a pan at a medium temperature. Use a cooking spray slightly.
5. Start on the pancakes and pour about ¼ of the batter onto the pan.
6. Once the pancake is firm and lightly browned on one side, flip each pancake to the other side.
7. Remove the cooked pancake from the pan. Keep cooking the pancakes until the batter is over.
8. Serve warm, and enjoy.

Nutritional value

Calories: 146kcal | Carbohydrates: 22g |Protein: 7g |Total Fat: 4g |Sugar: 5g |

Cholesterol: 2mg | Sodium: 209mg |Dietary Fiber: 3.1g | Saturated Fat: 0.5g |

Easy Peanut Butter Overnight Oats

Preparation Time: 5 min

Cooking Time: 5 hours | Servings: 2

Ingredients

1 cup old-rolled oats

1 tsp chia seeds

2 tbsps peanut butter

1 cup unsweetened almond milk

2 tbsps maple syrup

½ tsp vanilla

A pinch of sea salt

½ cup chopped peanuts

Mason jar

Preparation

1. Combine the oats, almond milk, peanut butter, maple syrup, chia seeds, vanilla, and a pinch of salt in a large bowl and stir well.
2. Divide the oat mixture into two mason jars with a lid and refrigerate overnight.
3. Add desired fruit toppings and chopped peanuts to enjoy when ready to eat.

Nutritional value

Calories: 380kcal | Carbohydrates: 48.6g |Protein: 15g |Total Fat: 16g |Sugar: 6.5g | Cholesterol: 8mg | Sodium: 259mg |Dietary Fiber: 7g | Saturated Fat: 3g |

Quinoa Veggie Collard Wraps

Preparation Time: 5 min

Cooking Time: 1 min | Servings: 4

Ingredients

4 collard leaves

½ cup of hummus (any variety)

1 cup cooked quinoa

1 medium cucumber

1 medium tomato

2 grated carrots

1 sliced avocado

½ cup of sprouts

Preparation

1. Begin by blanching the collard leaves. Fill a skillet 1 inch high with water. Bring the water to a boil, submerging the collard leaves one at a time, allowing them to cook for 15 - 20 seconds.
2. Move the leaves around in the water (flip if necessary until the whole leaf has turned bright green and is cooked. Repeat the process with the remaining leaves. Afterward, set aside and allow the leaves to cool completely.
3. When ready to assemble, carefully cut the stem out of the leaf. Start towards the top, and run your knife along the leaf's rib (being careful not to cut a hole itself). Cut to the bottom of the stem and cut the stem off.
4. To assemble, divide all the ingredients into four. Spread the hummus into the center of each leaf, then top with quinoa, cucumber, tomato, carrot, and sliced avocado and finish with the sprouts.
5. Fold the wraps in the sides, roll them as tightly as possible, and serve to enjoy.
6. Store the wraps whole and enjoy for 2 - 3 days.

Nutritional value

Calories: 218kcal | Carbohydrates: 25g |Protein: 7g |Total Fat: 12g |Sugar: 4g | Cholesterol: 8mg | Sodium: 149mg |Dietary

Fiber: 9g | Saturated Fat: 2g | Potassium: 687mg| Calcium: 72mg |

Breakfast Fruit Split

Preparation Time: 5 min

Cooking Time: 5 min | Servings: 4

Ingredients

1 small banana, peeled

½ cup of oat, corn, or granola cereal

½ cup low-fat vanilla or strawberry yogurt

½ tsp of honey (optional)

½ cup of canned pineapple chunks

Preparation

1. Cut the peeled banana lengthways. Place each piece in two cereal bowls. Add a dash of granola over the banana pieces and leave a little of the granola for further use.
2. Spread the yogurt on top of the granola. Add a bit of honey to the yogurt.
3. Top up with the extra granola and pineapple chunks.
4. Serve and enjoy!
5. Leftovers could be refrigerated within a 2-hour frame.

Nutritional value

Calories: 313kcal | Carbohydrates: 52.6g |Protein: 17.5g |Total Fat: 5.1g |Sugar: 33.2g | Cholesterol: 4.5mg |Dietary Fiber: 7.1g | Saturated Fat: 1.3g |

Eggs and Tomato Breakfast Melts

Preparation Time: 3 min

Cooking Time: 7 min | Servings: 4

Ingredients

2 whole-grain English muffins, split

2 ounces (about ½ cup) of low-fat Swiss cheese, shredded

½ cup grape or cherry heirloom tomatoes, quartered

1 tsp of olive oil

8 egg whites, whisked

4 scallions, finely chopped

Kosher salt, to taste

Black pepper, to taste

Preparation

1. Preheat the broiler on high. Place muffins, cut side up, on a baking sheet and broil for 2 minutes or until it begins to brown on the edges lightly. (your toaster oven is a great alternative).
2. Warm up a medium size skillet on medium heat. Add oil and sautée 3 scallions for about 2 to 3 minutes. Add the egg whites, season with salt and pepper, and cook, mixing with a wooden spoon until cooked through.
3. Divide on toasted muffins and top with tomatoes, cheese, and remaining scallions.
4. Broil for 1 to 1 ½ minutes or until the cheese has melted. Be careful not to burn.

Nutritional value

Calories: 160kcal | Carbohydrates: 16g |Protein: 15g |Total Fat: 5g |Sugar: 4g | Cholesterol: 8mg | Sodium: 329mg |Dietary Fiber: 3g | Saturated Fat: 0.5g |

Banana Oatmeal Pancakes

Preparation Time: 5 min

Cooking Time: 2 min | Servings: 6 pancakes

Ingredients

2 ripe bananas

2 eggs

1 cup oats

Toppings of your choice (vanilla, cinnamon, berries, nuts, etc.).

Preparation

1. Firstly, preheat a skillet on low heat.
2. Mix the bananas, eggs, and oats in a blender on low speed. Grease your skillet with cooking spray, oil, or butter, and pour the batter onto your prepared skillet (about ⅙ of the batter for each pancake). *Try flavoring your pancakes to taste with a pinch of salt, ½ tsp vanilla extract, or ½ tsp cinnamon*
3. Allow the pancakes to cook through on one side before flipping. If you use mix-ins like walnuts or blueberries, you can top them into the uncooked side of the pancakes before flipping. Mixing them with the batter may cause them to fall apart, so I don't recommend it.
4. Flip and cook the other side until done; repeat for the rest of the batter.
5. Serve with syrup, peanut butter, or your favorite pancake toppings.

Nutritional value

Calories: 241kcal | Carbohydrates: 41g |Protein: 9g |Total Fat: 5g |Sugar: 11g | Cholesterol: 123mg | Sodium: 50mg |Dietary Fiber: 5g | Saturated Fat: 1g |

Breakfast Triple Strata

Preparation Time: 10 min

Cooking Time: 50 min | Servings: 8

Ingredients

8 ounces of whole wheat bread

6 ounces of low-sodium turkey or chicken breakfast sausage

3 large eggs

12 ounces of egg substitute like egg beaters

1 medium russet potato (peel optional) cut into ¼-inch slices

2 cups fat-free milk

1 ½ cups of reduced-fat shredded sharp cheddar cheese

½ cup chopped green onions

1 cup sliced mushrooms

½ tsp paprika

Dash of ground black pepper

Preparation

1. First, preheat the oven to a temperature of 400°F.
2. Place the 1 inch of bread cubes on a baking tray. Bake for about 8-10 minutes until the cubes are slightly toasted.
3. Put the sausages in a pan and cook for 7-8 minutes until slightly browned.
4. Combine the cheese, eggs, milk, egg substitute, and spices in a separate bowl and stir using a whisk.
5. Mix well with the bread cubes, potatoes, sausage, mushrooms, and scallions.
6. Next, arrange the mixture in a baking tray. Cover with a lid and refrigerate for 8 hours. Subsequently, preheat the oven temperature to 350°F. Remove cover and bake for about 350°F.
7. Cut into pieces, and serve to enjoy.

Nutritional value

Calories: 289kcal | Carbohydrates: 18.2g |Protein: 24.3g |Total Fat: 12.4g |Sugar: 0.6g | Cholesterol: 86.7mg | Sodium: 355mg |Dietary Fiber: 1.3g | Saturated Fat: 1.8g |

Tropical Smoothie

Preparation Time: 5 min

Cooking Time: 1 min | Servings: 2

Ingredients

¾ cup frozen pineapple

¾ cup frozen mango

½ cup water

1 small frozen banana, chopped

1 ½ cups unsweetened coconut milk

1 tbsp coconut oil

3–4 ice cubes

Preparation

1. Place all the ingredients in a blender. Start blending on low, and as the contents break down, increase to medium speed until completely smooth, about 1 minute.

2. Serve immediately to enjoy.

Nutritional value

Calories: 219kcal | Carbohydrates: 30g |Protein: 1g |Total Fat: 11g |Sugar: 21g | Calcium: 1% | Sodium: 116mg |Dietary Fiber: 3g | Saturated Fat: 10g | Potassium: 362| Magnesium: 7% |

Egg Burrito

Preparation Time: 5 min

Cooking Time: 5 min | Servings: 1

Ingredients

2 tbsp chopped white onion

1 tbsp extra virgin olive oil

2 egg whites

1 whole egg

1 clove garlic, minced

1 cup spinach

¼ cup rinsed and drained canned black beans

⅛ cup shredded low-fat cheddar cheese

Cracked black pepper

1 100% whole wheat tortilla

1 tbsp chopped fresh cilantro

¼ cup chopped Roma tomato

1 tbsp prepared low-sodium salsa (optional)

Preparation

1. Heat the oil in a medium pan on medium heat. Add the garlic and the onion, and cook for about 30 seconds.

2. Whisk together the egg whites and whole egg. Add the eggs, spinach, cheese, and pepper to the pan and cook for 2 - 3 minutes or until the eggs are no longer runny. Then remove the pan from the heat.

3. Warm the tortilla in a flat pan over medium heat. Meanwhile, place the beans in a small pot, and bring them to a simmer. Set the warm tortilla on a plate, and spoon the beans into the middle of the tortilla in a line.

4. Add the vegetable and egg mixture, and top with cilantro, tomato, and salsa (if using).

5. Fold it into a burrito, and enjoy it immediately.

Nutritional value

Calories: 460kcal | Carbohydrates: 39g |Protein: 28g |Total Fat: 24g |Sugar: 21g | Cholesterol: 189mg | Sodium: 709mg |Dietary Fiber: 9g | Saturated Fat: 4g | Potassium: 518mg | Magnesium: 16% | Calcium: 14%.

Peachy Green Shake

Preparation Time: 5 min

Cooking Time: 5 min | Servings: 6

Ingredients

1 tbsp coconut oil

2 cups spinach

1 cup water

½ cup frozen strawberries

1 ½ cups frozen peach

1 small frozen banana, chopped

Preparation

1. Place the spinach and water in a blender and blend on low. As the spinach breaks down, increase to medium speed until completely smooth.

2. Add the fruit and coconut oil, and blend on medium to high speed until desired consistency is achieved about 1 minute. Serve immediately.

Nutritional value

Calories: 178kcal | Carbohydrates: 30g |Protein: 3g |Total Fat: 7g |Sugar: 8g | Cholesterol: 44mg | Sodium: 27mg |Dietary Fiber: 5g | Saturated Fat: 6g | Potassium: 682mg |

English Muffin with Berries

Preparation Time: 15 min

Cooking Time: 20 min | Servings: 12 muffins

Ingredients

2 cups all-purpose flour

1/4 cup sugar

2 teaspoons baking powder

1/2 teaspoon baking soda

1/2 teaspoon salt

1/2 cup unsweetened applesauce

1/2 cup low-fat milk

1/4 cup vegetable oil

2 eggs

1 teaspoon vanilla extract

1 cup mixed berries (fresh or frozen)

Preparation

1. Preheat the oven to 375°F.

2. Whisk together the flour, baking soda, sugar, baking powder, and salt in a large bowl.

3. Whisk together the applesauce, milk, vegetable oil, eggs, and vanilla extract in another bowl.

4. Add wet ingredients to the dry ones and stir.

5. Add mixed berries.

6. Pour the batter into the muffin cans and bake them for 18-20 minutes.

7. Cool muffins for 5 minutes before serving.

Nutritional value

Calories: 160 kcal | Carbohydrates: 23g |Protein: 3g |Total Fat: 7g |Sugar: 6g | Cholesterol: 30mg | Sodium: 140mg |Dietary Fiber: 1g | Saturated Fat: 1g |

Protein Bowl

Preparation Time: 5 min

Cooking Time: 5 min | Servings: 6

Ingredients

1 tbsp almond butter

¼ cup uncooked old-fashioned oats

¾ cup low-fat cottage cheese

½ medium banana, thinly sliced

Preparation

1. All the ingredients mix in a small bowl and enjoy.

Nutritional value

Calories: 346kcal | Carbohydrates: 47g |Protein: 28g |Total Fat: 12g |Sugar: 8g | Cholesterol: 7mg | Sodium: 690mg |Dietary Fiber: 9g | Saturated Fat: 2g | Potassium: 547mg |

Apples and Cinnamon Oatmeal

Preparation Time: 10 min

Cooking Time: 5 min | Servings: 2

Ingredients

1 ½ cups unsweetened plain almond milk

1 cup of old-fashioned oats

1 large unpeeled Granny Smith apple, cubed

¼ tsp ground cinnamon

2 tbsps toasted walnut pieces

Preparation

1. Bring the milk to a simmer on medium heat, and add the oats and apple. Stir until most of the liquid is absorbed for about 4 minutes.

2. Stir in the cinnamon. Serve the oatmeal mixture and top with walnuts.

Nutritional value

Calories: 377kcal | Carbohydrates: 73g |Protein: 13g |Total Fat: 16g |Sugar: 17g | Cholesterol: 44mg | Sodium: 77mg |Dietary Fiber: 11g | Saturated Fat: 2g | Potassium: 399mg |

Energy Oatmeal

Preparation Time: 10 min

Cooking Time: 5 min | Servings: 1

Ingredients

½ cup old-fashioned oats

¼ cup water

¼ cup low-fat milk

¼ cup blueberries

4 egg whites, beaten

⅛ tsp ground cinnamon

⅛ tsp ground ginger

Preparation

1. Heat the water and milk to a simmer on medium heat in a small pot. Add the oats, constantly stirring for about 4 minutes.

2. Add the beaten egg whites gradually, stirring constantly. Cook for 5 minutes or until the eggs are no longer runny.

3. Stir the cinnamon and ginger into the oatmeal mixture, and scoop the mixture into a bowl.

4. Top with berries and serve.

Nutritional value

Calories: 270kcal | Carbohydrates: 60g |Protein: 23g |Total Fat: 4g |Sugar: 7g | Cholesterol: 5mg | Sodium: 250mg |Dietary Fiber: 9g | Saturated Fat: 2g | Potassium: 371mg | Calcium: 14%.

Veggie and Egg Breakfast Bowl

Preparation Time: 15 min

Cooking Time: 15 min | Servings: 2

Ingredients

2 cups chopped kale

½cup sliced mushrooms

½cup chopped red bell pepper

¼cup diced onion

1 clove garlic, minced

4 large eggs

1 tbsp olive oil

¼tsp black pepper

½ avocado, sliced

Preparation

1. Heat the olive oil in a large skillet on medium heat. Onion and garlic add to the skillet and cook for 2 - 3 minutes until they soften.

2. Add kale, mushrooms, and red bell pepper to the skillet and cook for 3 - 4 minutes until the vegetables are tender.

3. Crack the eggs into the skillet and add black pepper on top. Cook the eggs for 3 - 4 minutes until the egg whites are firm, yet the yolks remain soft and runny.

4. Serve in bowls and top with sliced avocado.

Nutritional value

Calories: 230kcal | Carbohydrates: 12g |Protein: 13g |Total Fat: 16g |Sugar: 3g | Cholesterol: 186mg | Sodium: 65mg |Dietary Fiber: 5g | Saturated Fat: 3g

DASH Diet Soup Recipes

Here you'll find rich and nutritious soups to fill your belly and improve your overall health.

Beef Stew with Fennel & Shallots

Preparation Time: 30 min

Cooking Time: 2 hrs| Servings: 6

Ingredients

1 pound boneless lean beef

3 mushrooms, chopped

½ fennel bulb

3 tbsp of flour

4 potatoes, chopped

2 tbsp olive oil

3 large shallots, chopped

⅓ cup chopped fresh parsley

2 fresh thyme sprigs

4 carrots, sliced

¾ tsp of ground pepper

1 bay leaf

10 boiling onions

2 cloves garlic

3 cups of low-sodium broth or vegetable stock

½ cup red wine (optional)

Preparation

1. First, prepare your beef by trimming any visible fat and cutting it into cubes. Next, pour your flour on a plate and coat your beef cubes in the flour.

2. Get a large saucepan and heat oil over medium heat.

3. Then, add the beef and cook for 5 minutes until browned on all sides. Once done, remove the beef from the heat and set aside.

4. Add the fennel, garlic, and shallots over medium heat in the same saucepan and saute for 8 minutes until softened. Next, add salt, pepper, thyme sprigs, and bay leaf and saute for another 1 minute.

5. Add the precooked beef to the pan, pour your broth and wine, and simmer for 45 minutes on low heat until the meat is tender.

6. Next, add the carrots, mushrooms, potatoes, and onions and simmer for 30 min until the vegetables are tender. Once done, remove the bay leaf and thyme sprigs. Add in the parsley and serve.

Nutritional value

Calories: 244kcal | Carbohydrates: 22g |Protein: 21g |Total Fat: 8.5g |Sugar: 10g | Cholesterol: 44mg | Sodium: 185mg |Dietary Fiber: 4.5g | Saturated Fat: 2g | Potassium: 518mg | Calcium: 14%.

Chicken and Spinach Soup with Fresh Pesto

Preparation Time: 10 min

Cooking Time: 30 min | Servings: 1

Ingredients

4-pound chicken breast

2 tsp olive oil

½ cup carrot

½ cup red bell pepper

1 clove garlic, minced

¼ cup grated Parmesan cheese

1 tsp dried marjoram

½ cup croutons

2 cups low-sodium chicken broth

3 ounces spinach

1 cup white beans

⅓ cup fresh basil leaves

Ground pepper

Preparation

1. Heat 2 tbsps of oil in a large saucepan on medium heat. Add chicken, carrot, garlic, and bell pepper, and cook for 4 minutes until the chicken begins to brown on all sides.

2. Add the stock and marjoram, and boil on medium heat while frequently stirring until the chicken is cooked.

3. Next, transfer the chicken pieces to a chopping board and cool before dicing them into bite sizes. In the same pan, add the spinach and beans. Allow cooking for 5 minutes until the flavors are blended.

4. Finally, add the chopped chicken and the pesto into the pot and season with pepper. Simmer until hot. Garnish with croutons, and serve.

Nutritional value

Calories: 227kcal | Carbohydrates: 18g |Protein: 19.4g |Total Fat: 9g |Sugar: 1.7g | Cholesterol: 83.5mg | Sodium: 211mg |Dietary Fiber: 20.1g | Saturated Fat: 26g | Potassium: 524.6mg | Magnesium: 4mg4| Calcium: 385mg

Classic Chicken Noodle Soup

Preparation Time: 10 min

Cooking Time: 10 min | Servings: 6

Ingredients

2 ounces uncooked, extra-wide egg noodles

4 cups low-sodium chicken broth

½ pound boneless, skinless chicken breast

About ½ cup, two carrots peeled and chopped

1 stalk celery, sliced

Cracked pepper

Cilantro for garnish

Preparation

1. Season the chicken with pepper and salt. Add the chicken, noodles, carrot, celery, and broth to your instant pot.

2. Cook on high heat for 5 minutes.

3. Once done, remove the chicken from the pot. Shred it and returned it to the pot.

4. Season to your taste with cracked pepper. You can also add red chili flakes for more spice. Add cilantro and fresh mint for herby taste.

5. Serve hot to enjoy.

Nutritional value

Calories: 773kcal | Carbohydrates: 66.1g |Protein: 48.6g |Total Fat: 35.4g |Sugar: 9.7g | Cholesterol: 117.5mg | Sodium: 1741.9mg |Dietary Fiber: 9.6g | Saturated Fat: 6.6g | Potassium: 873.6mg | Calcium: 27.8mg |

Hearty Chicken Soup

Preparation Time: 20 min

Cooking Time: 25 min | Servings: 6

Ingredients

1 ½ lbs boneless chicken breast

1 cup wild rice

2 cups chopped onions

2 cups chopped carrots

2 cups chopped celery

4 garlic cloves

1 cup green beans

2 bay leaves

¼ tsp ground black pepper

12 cups organic chicken broth

1 cup chopped parsley leaves

Preparation

1. Place all the ingredients, except chopped parsley, in a slow cooker and cook for 4 hours on high heat.
2. Remove chicken and shred with the help of two forks.
3. Return chicken to the soup and top with fresh parsley.
4. Serve hot to enjoy.

Nutritional value

Calories: 314kcal | Carbohydrates: 25g |Protein: 31g |Total Fat: 10g |Cholesterol: 104mg | Sodium: 606mg |Dietary Fiber: 4g | Saturated Fat: 2.1g | Calcium: 80mg |

Chicken Pasta Soup

Preparation Time: 2 min
Cooking Time: 22 min | Servings: 6

Ingredients

4 cups low-sodium chicken broth

1 tsp olive oil

1 cup chopped onion

3 cloves garlic, minced

1 cup celery

1 carrot

4-ounce dried linguini

1 skinless chicken breast, cut into desired size

2 tbsps fresh parsley

Preparation

1. First, heat the olive oil in a large pot on medium heat and saute the onions and garlic. Add the sliced carrots and celery and saute for a few minutes.
2. In the same pot, add the chicken broth and bring it to a boil. After a while, reduce the heat, cover the saucepan, and simmer for 5 minutes.

3. Stir in the linguini and return to medium heat for 10 min until pasta and vegetables are tender; ensure to stir occasionally.
4. Add the cooked chicken and fresh parsley to the pot and allow to heat through. Serve hot to enjoy.

Nutritional value

Calories: 156kcal | Carbohydrates: 13g |Protein: 20g |Total Fat: 3g |Sugar: 8.6g | Cholesterol: 40mg | Sodium: 723mg |Dietary Fiber: 3g | Saturated Fat: 0.6g |

Creamy Asparagus Soup

Preparation Time: 15 min
Cooking Time: 30 min | Servings: 6

Ingredients

2 cups peeled and diced potatoes

½ cup whole-wheat (whole-meal) flour

½ pound fresh asparagus cut into 1/4-inch pieces

½ cup chopped onion

2 stalks of celery, chopped

4 cups water

2 tablespoons butter

1 ½ cups fat-free milk

Lemon zest, to taste

Cracked black pepper, to taste

Preparation

1. Combine the potatoes, asparagus, onions, celery, and water in a large soup pot and set high heat. Bring to a boil. Reduce heat, cover, and simmer until the vegetables are tender for about 15 minutes.
2. Next, stir in the butter.
3. In a small bowl, whisk the flour and milk. Pour the mixture slowly into the soup pot,

stirring constantly. Increase the heat to medium-high and stir for about 5 minutes until the soup thickens.

4. Remove from heat. Add lemon zest and cracked black pepper to taste.

5. Serve in warm bowls to enjoy.

Nutritional value

Calories: 140kcal | Carbohydrates: 22g |Protein: 6g |Total Fat: 4g |Sugar: 0g | Cholesterol: 11mg | Sodium: 76mg |Dietary Fiber: 3g | Saturated Fat: 3g |

Cauliflower Carrot Soup

Preparation Time: 15 min

Cooking Time: 30 min| Servings: 6

Ingredients

1 large head cauliflower, coarsely chopped

2 tbsp olive oil

½ small white onion, chopped

2 large cloves garlic, chopped

½ tsp cracked black pepper

⅛ tsp chile pepper flakes

⅛ tsp dried basil

1 cup chopped carrot

1-quart low-sodium vegetable broth

½ tsp salt

Preparation

1. Boil water in a large pot. Then, remove the cauliflower head's outer leaves, coarsely chop the cauliflower, and add it to the boiling water.

2. Cover the pot, and allow to boil for 6 or 8 minutes, or until a fork easily pierces the cauliflower pieces. Strain the cauliflower, and discard the water.

3. Heat the oil in the same pot over medium heat. Add the onion, garlic, and carrot, and saute until the onion is translucent. Add the cauliflower. Transfer veggies to a blender, add 1 cup of broth, and blend until smooth.

4. Once done, transfer the blended veggies to another large pot. Heat the mixed veggies over medium-high heat, and season with salt, pepper, chile pepper flakes, and basil.

5. Bring to a boil, and serve hot to enjoy.

Nutritional value

Calories: 106kcal | Carbohydrates: 53.8g |Protein: 4g |Total Fat: 5g |Sugar: 3g | Cholesterol: 0mg | Sodium: 409mg |Dietary Fiber: 5g | Saturated Fat: 3g | Potassium: 498mg

Roasted Butternut Squash Soup

Preparation Time: 15 min

Cooking Time: 40 min | Servings: 6

Ingredients

1 large butternut squash

2 tbsps olive oil

2 ½ liters low-sodium vegetable or chicken broth

⅛ tsp cracked black pepper

¼ tsp white pepper

1 tbsp chopped fresh parsley

1 large clove of garlic

½ white onion, chopped

¼ tsp chile pepper flakes

1 tsp finely chopped fresh rosemary

3 minced fresh sage leaves

Preparation

1. Preheat the oven to 400°F. Cut through the squash and scoop out the seeds from the center until no strings or seeds are left.
2. Coat a baking sheet with the olive oil spray, and place the squash on it. After that, roast in the oven for 30 minutes or until the squash is soft. Afterward, take it off the oven, and let it cool completely.
3. Add the oil, garlic, and onion in a large pot over medium heat. Saute for a few minutes until the onion turns light brown. Meanwhile, scoop out the roasted squash, add to the pot, and mix.
4. Add the broth, and boil on low heat. Transfer the veggies to a blender, leaving the most liquid in the pot. Blend the squash on low to mix, then on high until smooth.
5. Once all the squash has been blended, please return it to the pot, and add the rest of the broth and the black pepper, white pepper, parsley, chili pepper flakes, rosemary, and sage. Bring to a boil and serve.

Nutritional value

Calories: 158kcal | Carbohydrates: 19.2g |Protein: 3g |Total Fat: 6g |Sugar: 5g | Cholesterol: 0mg | Sodium: 699mg |Dietary Fiber: 6g | Saturated Fat: 1.8g | Potassium: 425mg |

Mushroom Barley Soup

Preparation Time: 15 min
Cooking Time: 40 min | Servings: 9
Ingredients
8 cups vegetable stock
½ small potato, chopped
¼ cup thinly sliced green onions

1 tbsp canola oil
1 ½ cups chopped onions
1 cup sliced mushrooms
¾ cup chopped carrots
1 tsp dried thyme
⅛ tsp black pepper
½ tsp chopped garlic
¾ cup pearl barley
3 ounces dry sherry

Preparation

1. Heat the oil in a large pot. Then, add the onions, mushrooms, carrots, thyme, pepper, and garlic. Saute for 5 minutes until the onion is translucent.
2. Next, add the vegetable stock and barley and bring them to a boil. Decrease heat and simmer for 20 minutes or until the barley is tender. Stir in sherry and potato. Continue to simmer until the potato is cooked, about 15 minutes.
3. Garnish with sliced green onions and serve to enjoy.

Nutritional value

Calories: 121kcal | Carbohydrates: 19g |Protein: 2g |Total Fat: 4g |Sugar: 2g | Cholesterol: 0mg | Sodium: 112mg |Dietary Fiber: 2g | Saturated Fat: 0g |

White Turkey Chili

Preparation Time: 20 min
Cooking Time: 30 min | Servings: 6
Ingredients
4 cups low-sodium chicken broth
1 pound ground turkey
3 tbsps olive oil
1 large onion, diced

4 cloves garlic, minced

¼ tsp salt

2 cans of low-sodium white beans

2 cans of green chiles

2 medium zucchini, diced

2 tbsps dried oregano

1 tbsp ground cumin

½ tsp ground coriander

½ tsp white pepper

Preparation

1. Add ground turkey, onion, and garlic to the large pot and cook for 10 minutes on medium-high heat until turkey is browned on all sides. Then, stir in the zucchini and cook for 5 minutes until the vegetable softens.

2. Next, add the oregano, cumin, coriander, white pepper, and salt and stir for 5 minutes. Afterward, add the white beans, chiles, and broth and allow to simmer for 10 minutes.

Nutritional value

Calories: 396kcal | Carbohydrates: 27g |Protein: 28.2g |Total Fat: 17g |Sugar: 2g | Cholesterol: 43.3mg | Sodium: 595.6mg |Dietary Fiber: 10.1g | Saturated Fat: 2.7g | Potassium: 999.5mg | Magnesium: 41.2mg| Calcium: 303mg |

Zucchini Soup

Preparation Time: 15 min

Cooking Time: 20 min | Servings: 6

Ingredients

4 zucchini, sliced

2 tbsp extra-virgin olive oil

2 potatoes, cubed

1 onion, chopped

2 cloves garlic, crushed

4c low sodium vegetable broth

2 carrots, sliced

1 tsp dried basil

Black pepper, to taste

Preparation

1. Plate all the ingredients into your slow cooker.

2. Cover to cook for 20 minutes or until veggies are tender.

3. Serve to enjoy.

Nutritional value

Calories: 136kcal | Carbohydrates: 21g |Protein: 3g |Total Fat: 5g| Sodium: 55mg |

Minestrone Soup

Preparation Time: 15 min

Cooking Time: 30 min | Servings: 3

Ingredients

4 cups low-sodium chicken broth

2 tbsp basil, fresh

1 carrot

⅓ stalk celery, diced

1 garlic clove, minced

½ cup onion, chopped

½ cup spinach, chopped

2 large tomatoes, chopped

1 zucchini, small

½ cup elbow pasta

1 tbsp extra virgin Olive oil

Preparation

1. Heat the olive oil in a large saucepan. Then, add the onion, celery, garlic, and carrots and cook until softened for about 5 minutes.

2. Stir in the beans, basil, broth, tomatoes, spinach, and pasta. Bring to a boil over high heat. Reduce heat and simmer for 10 minutes.

3. Add zucchini and cover to cook until tender.

4. Top with parmesan and serve to enjoy.

Nutritional value

Calories: 260kcal | Carbohydrates: 37g |Protein: 15g |Total Fat: 8g |Sugar: 12.1g | Cholesterol: 0mg | Sodium: 560mg |Dietary Fiber: 10g | Saturated Fat: 1.0g | Potassium: 841mg |

Wild Rice Mushroom Soup

Preparation Time: 40 min

Cooking Time: 40 min | Servings: 4

Ingredients

1 cup cooked wild rice

1 tbsp olive oil

Half a white onion, chopped

1 ½ cups sliced fresh white mushrooms

½ cup white wine, or 1/2 cup low-sodium, fat-free chicken broth

¼ cup chopped celery

¼ cup chopped carrots

2 ½ cups low-sodium, fat-free chicken broth

1 cup fat-free half-and-half

2 tbsp flour

¼ tsp dried thyme

Black pepper

Preparation

1. Put olive oil in a stockpot and bring to medium heat. Add chopped onion, celery, and carrots. Cook until tender. Add mushrooms, white wine, and chicken broth. Cover and heat through.
2. In a bowl, blend half-and-half, flour, thyme, and pepper. Then stir in cooked wild rice.
3. Pour the rice mixture into a hot stockpot with vegetables. Cook over medium heat. Stir continually until thickened and bubbly.

4. Serve warm to enjoy.

Nutritional value

Calories: 173kcal | Carbohydrates: 22g |Protein: 13.2g |Total Fat: 5g |Sugar: 6g | Cholesterol: 4mg | Sodium: 113mg |Dietary Fiber: 2g | Saturated Fat: 1g | Potassium: 437mg |

Steamy Salmon Chowder

Preparation Time: 10 min

Cooking Time: 30 min | Servings: 8

Ingredients

½ tsp dill

½ tsp ground pepper

6 ounces salmon

1 can of low-sodium creamed corn

½ cup chopped celery

1 tsp olive oil

1 can of fat-free evaporated milk

1 clove garlic, minced

2 ½ cups hash browns

1 can chicken broth

1 cup frozen peas and carrots

Preparation

1. First, heat the olive oil in a large pot and saute the celery and garlic for 10 minutes.
2. Combine the chicken broth, hash browns, carrots, peas, dill, and pepper, and allow the mixture to cook for 10 minutes until the vegetables are tender.
3. Stir in the salmon, evaporated milk, and corn and cook until heated.

Nutritional value

Calories: 490kcal | Carbohydrates: 22g |Protein: 11g |Total Fat: 2.5g |Sugar: 9g |

Cholesterol: 18mg | Sodium: 450mg |Dietary Fiber: 2g | Saturated Fat: 0.5g |

Cholesterol: 24mg | Sodium: 227mg |Dietary Fiber: 6g | Saturated Fat: 5g |

Broccoli Soup

Preparation Time: 20 min

Cooking Time: 40 min | Servings: 4

Ingredients

3 cups low-sodium chicken broth

⅛ tsp chile pepper flakes

¼ tsp cracked black pepper

8 cups coarsely chopped broccoli

2 tbsps extra virgin olive oil

1 cup chopped white onion

2 large cloves of garlic

½ cup low-fat milk

Preparation

1. Boil water in a large pot. Add the broccoli, and boil for about 8 - 10 minutes. Drain the broccoli, and set aside.

2. In the same pot, heat the oil on medium heat. Next, add the onion and garlic, and cook for 2 minutes, stirring until the onion is translucent.

3. Add the cooked broccoli and the broth to the pot, and simmer for another 4 to 5 minutes. Turn off the heat, transfer the veggies and a little broth in small batches to a blender, and blend until smooth.

4. Pour the blended soup into another pot, and repeat until the broccoli mixture has been mixed. Add chile pepper flakes, black pepper, and milk to the soup, and boil. Dish into bowls and serve to enjoy.

Nutritional value

Calories: 291kcal | Carbohydrates: 28g |Protein: 17g |Total Fat: 5g |Sugar: 14g |

Pesto Chicken & Cannellini Bean Soup

Preparation Time: 20 min

Cooking Time: 40 min | Servings: 8

Ingredients

2 pounds skinless chicken breasts

1 tbsp fresh oregano, chopped

1 tbsp fresh marjoram

3 cups broccolini

8 cups chicken broth

¼ cup prepared pesto

3 cups sliced fennel

2 tbsp olive oil

1 can cannellini beans

2 large cloves garlic, minced

2 cups tomatoes, chopped

1 onion, chopped

Salt to taste

½ tsp ground pepper

Preparation

1. Saute your onion, pepper, and garlic and cook for 3 minutes in a large pot over medium heat. At this point, add in the oregano and marjoram and allow to cook for an additional 1 minute.

2. Add the low-sodium chicken broth and chicken and allow to simmer for 22 minutes. Ensure to turn the chicken from time to time until its tender.

3. Once ready, transfer the chicken to a cutting board and shred the meat off the bone. Meanwhile, add fennel, broccolini, and

tomatoes to the pot and cook for 10 minutes until the vegetables are tender.

4. Add the shredded chicken, beans, salt, and pepper and cook for 3 minutes until heated. Once done, stir in pesto and enjoy.

Nutritional value

Calories: 469kcal | Carbohydrates: 64g |Protein: 25g |Total Fat: 13g |Sugar: 5g | Cholesterol: 47.6mg | Sodium: 606mg |Dietary Fiber: 4.4g | Saturated Fat: 2.5g | Potassium: 806.3mg | Magnesium: 57.8mg| Calcium: 133.7mg |

Moroccan Chicken & Sweet Potato Soup

Preparation Time: 15 min

Cooking Time: 40 min | Servings: 8

Ingredients

2 pounds of boneless chicken breast

2 tbsp olive oil

1 cup onion

2 large cloves garlic, minced

3 cups sweet potato, diced

8 cups chicken broth

2 cups chopped red bell pepper

2 cups green beans

1 ½ tsp ground cumin

½ tsp ground cinnamon

¼ tsp cayenne pepper

1 can chickpeas

½ tsp salt

½ tsp ground pepper

Preparation

1. First, heat the olive oil in a large pot and saute onion and garlic for 2 minutes. Then, add cumin, cinnamon, and cayenne, and cook for 1

minute before adding the chicken and the stock. Allow cooking 20 to 22 minutes while turning occasionally.

2. Once done, transfer the chicken to a chopping board and shred the chicken into pieces. Next, add sweet potato, bell pepper, and green beans in the same pot and simmer until the vegetables are tender. Add the shredded chicken, chickpeas, pepper, and salt to taste and cook for 3 minutes until heated.

Nutritional value

Calories: 268kcal | Carbohydrates: 27g |Protein: 25g |Total Fat: 8g |Sugar: 5.6g | Cholesterol: 45.1mg | Sodium: 585mg |Dietary Fiber: 5.6g | Saturated Fat: 1.5g | Potassium: 794.4mg | Magnesium: 60.3mg|

Zesty Tomato Soup

Preparation Time: 5 min

Cooking Time: 15 min | Servings: 2

Ingredients

1 medium tomato, chopped

2 tsp croutons

1 tbsp parmesan cheese, grated

1 can condensed low-sodium, low-fat tomato soup

1 can of fat-free milk

1 tbsp chopped fresh basil

Preparation

1. Add the low-fat tomato soup and milk to a saucepan and stir on medium heat for 10 minutes until smooth. Add the chopped tomato and herbs and cook for 5 minutes, stirring occasionally.

2. Garnish each serving with 1 tbsp of croutons and 1 ½ teaspoons Parmesan cheese.

Nutritional value

Calories: 45kcal | Carbohydrates: 11g |Protein: 9g |Total Fat: 2g |Sugar: 7g | Cholesterol: 5mg | Sodium: 220mg |Dietary Fiber: 3g | Saturated Fat: 1g |

Pumpkin Soup

Preparation Time: 10 min

Cooking Time: 20 min | Servings: 4

Ingredients

1 cup fat-free milk

1 green onion top, chopped

⅛ tsp black pepper

1 can (15 ounces) pumpkin puree

2 cups low-sodium vegetable broth

½ tsp ground cinnamon

1 small onion, chopped

¼ tsp ground nutmeg

Preparation

1. Heat the olive oil on medium heat in a large saucepan. Then, add onion and garlic and cook for 3 minutes until tender.
2. Add the pumpkin puree, broth, cinnamon, and nutmeg, and boil.
3. Reduce heat, and simmer for 5 minutes. Stir in the milk and cook until hot.
4. Serve warm and garnish with black pepper and green onion.

Nutritional value

Calories: 291kcal | Carbohydrates: 13g |Protein: 3g |Total Fat: 23.8g |Sugar: 7g | Cholesterol: 1mg | Sodium: 379mg |Dietary Fiber: 2.5g | Saturated Fat: 1g |

Veggie Pasta Soup

Preparation Time: 35 min

Cooking Time: 35 min | Servings: 12

Ingredients

1 pound low-sodium chicken broth

1 cup thinly sliced celery

4 cups water

1 ½ cups dried ditalini pasta

2 tbsps olive oil

6 cloves garlic, minced

1 ½ cups coarsely shredded carrot

1 cup chopped onion

½ cup shaved Parmesan cheese

2 tbsps fresh parsley

Preparation

1. Heat the olive oil in a pot on medium heat. Add the minced garlic and cook for a minute. Stir onion, celery, and carrot, and cook until tender.
2. Pour in the water and chicken broth and bring it to a boil. Add the pasta and allow to cook until the pasta is soft.
3. Serve in pasta bowls and top with parsley and parmesan cheese.

Nutritional value

Calories: 86kcal | Carbohydrates: 15g |Protein: 4g |Total Fat: 2g |Potassium: 128g | Cholesterol: 0.5mg | Sodium: 227mg |Dietary Fiber: 1g | Saturated Fat: 0g |

Slow Cooker Pot Pea and Ham Soup

Preparation Time: 20 min

Cooking Time: 4 hours | Servings: 12

Ingredients

1 pound bag of dried split peas

1-2 tbsp soft and savory spices to taste

1 cup celery, sliced

1 cup carrots, sliced

1 cup Onion, sliced

2 cups diced cooked low-sodium ham,

6-8 cup Water

Preparation

1. Add the split peas, celery, carrots, onion, cooked ham, water, and spices in a slow cooker.

2. Cover, and cook on a high heat setting for 4 to 5 hours.

3. Serve hot in bowls.

Nutritional value

Calories: 213kcal | Carbohydrates: 42g |Protein: 4g |Total Fat: 1g |Potassium: 128g | Cholesterol: 0.5mg | Sodium: 598mg |Dietary Fiber: 8g | Saturated Fat: 0g |

DASH Diet Salads

I have curated the following salad recipes full of veggies, fruits, and healthy proteins to boost your metabolism and improve your heart health. Enjoy.

Chicken Pasta Salad

Preparation Time: 25 min

Cooking Time: 15 min | Servings: 4

Ingredients

1 (6-ounce) boneless, skinless chicken breast

8 ounces of whole-wheat penne pasta

½ cup low-fat plain Greek yogurt

1 cup halved seedless red grapes

¼ cup walnut pieces

1 tbsp red wine vinegar

½ cup chopped celery

½ tsp cracked black pepper

⅛ tsp sea salt

Preparation

1. Boil a large pot of water, add the pasta, and stir. Cook for 8 - 10 minutes. Once ready, strain the pasta.

2. While the pasta is cooking, trim the fat off the chicken, if any, and cut it into small cubes. Fill a separate, medium pot with water, and boil it over high heat. Add the chicken cubes (water should cover them), and cook for 5 to 6 minutes. Once done, drain the chicken.

3. In a large bowl, combine the pasta and the chicken with the remaining ingredients, and mix well. Refrigerate for 20 to 30 minutes before serving to enjoy.

Nutritional value

Calories: 115kcal | Carbohydrates: 11g |Protein: 10g |Total Fat: 4g |Sugar: 3g | Cholesterol: 16mg | Sodium: 84mg |Dietary Fiber: 2g | Saturated Fat: 0.5g | Potassium: 165 | Calcium: 4% |

Shrimp, Cherry Tomato & Asparagus Salad

Preparation Time: 5 min

Cooking Time: 18 min | Servings: 4

Ingredients

1 16-ounce. package frozen peeled, cooked shrimp with tails intact, thawed

12-ounce fresh asparagus spears trimmed

Black pepper

Wheat Cracker bread (optional)

4 cups watercress, tough stems removed

2 cups cherry tomatoes, halved

½ cup bottled light raspberry or berry vinaigrette salad dressing cracked

Preparation

1. Cover the asparagus in a small amount of lightly boiling, salted water in a large skillet and cook until crisp and tender.

2. Drain in a colander and run the cooked asparagus under cold water until it cools.

3. Divide the asparagus on your plate, top it with shrimp, cherry tomatoes, and watercress, and drizzle with salad dressing.

4. Sprinkle cracked black pepper on top and serve with wheat cracker bread to enjoy.

Nutritional value

Calories: 213kcal | Carbohydrates: 12g |Protein: 20g |Total Fat: 12g |Sugar: 7g |

Cholesterol: 149mg | Sodium: 268mg |Dietary Fiber: 4g | Saturated Fat: 1g |

Pomegranate Salad

Preparation Time: 10 min

Cooking Time: 10 min | Servings: 4

Ingredients

4 cups arugula

1 large avocado, chopped

¼ cup pomegranate seeds

½ cup thinly sliced fennel

½ cup thinly sliced Anjou pears, thinly sliced

Preparation

1. In a large bowl, mix all the ingredients.
2. Add the pomegranate seeds last.
3. Toss well, and serve with your favorite oil and vinegar dressing.

Nutritional value

Calories: 106 kcal | Carbohydrates: 12g |Protein: 2g |Total Fat: 7g |Sugar: 4g | Cholesterol: 0mg | Sodium: 15mg |Dietary Fiber: 4g |

Asian Vegetable Salad

Preparation Time: 20 min

Cooking Time: 5 min | Servings: 4

Ingredients

1 ½ cups thinly sliced spinach

1 tbsp thinly sliced cilantro

1 ½ cup julienned carrot

½ cup julienned red bell pepper

1 ½ cup julienned bok choy

½ cup julienned yellow onion

1 cup thinly sliced red cabbage

1 tbsp minced garlic

1 ½ tbsps chopped cashews

1 ½ cups snow peas

2 tsp toasted sesame oil

2 tsp low-sodium soy sauce

Preparation

1. Rinse all vegetables under cold running water and allow them to drain.
2. Cut the carrot, pepper, bok choy, and onion into skinny strips.
3. Cut across the grain into little cabbage, spinach, and cilantro strips.
4. Next, toss the cut vegetables, garlic, cashews, and snow peas in a large bowl. Drizzle sesame oil and soy sauce over the salad. Toss again to combine.
5. Serve to enjoy.

Nutritional value

Calories: 113 kcal | Carbohydrates: 14g |Protein: 3g |Total Fat: 4g |Sugar: 6g | Cholesterol: 0mg | Sodium: 168mg |Dietary Fiber: 4g | Saturated Fat: 1 |

Greek Salad with Lemon Vinaigrette

Preparation Time: 10 min

Cooking Time: 10 min | Servings: 4

Ingredients

1 tsp dried oregano

10 black olives, chopped

8 tablespoons lemon Vinaigrette

4 cups chopped romaine leaves

½ cup cherry tomatoes

½ cup coarsely chopped canned artichoke hearts

¼ cup low-fat feta cheese

Preparation

1. Mix all the ingredients in a large bowl, and toss well.

2. Serve with 2 tablespoons of lemon vinaigrette on the side.

Nutritional value

Calories: 173 kcal | Carbohydrates: 4g | Protein: 0.1g | Total Fat: 19g | Sugar: 3g | Cholesterol: 2mg | Sodium: 49mg | Dietary Fiber: 0.1g | Saturated Fat: 3|

Couscous Salad

Preparation Time: 10 min

Cooking Time: 10 min | Servings: 8

Ingredients

2 tbsps olive oil

1 cup zucchini

1 cup whole wheat couscous

1 medium red bell pepper

1 tbsp lemon juice

⅓ cup parsley, chopped

½ cup red onion, chopped

¾ tsp ground cumin

½ tsp ground black pepper

Preparation

1. In a large bowl, add water and a pinch of salt to cook the couscous. Once cooked, fluff with a fork and allow to cool. Add the zucchini, bell pepper, onion, cumin, and black pepper, and set aside.

2. Mix olive oil and lemon juice in another bowl and pour the couscous mixture. Toss to combine and garnish with herbs to enjoy.

Nutritional value

Calories: 340kcal | Carbohydrates: 21g | Protein: 4g | Total Fat: 4g | Sugar: 6g |

Cholesterol: 19mg | Sodium: 3mg | Dietary Fiber: 3g | Saturated Fat: 0.5 |

Healthy Cobb Salad with Basic Vinaigrette

Preparation Time: 10 min

Cooking Time: 10 min | Servings: 4

Ingredients

5 cups spinach

4 slices of turkey bacon

1 cup sliced cremini mushrooms

½ cup shredded carrot

⅓ cup crumbled blue cheese

Basic Vinaigrette

½ large cucumber, sliced

½ (15-ounce) can of kidney beans

1 large avocado, pitted, peeled, and chopped

Preparation

1. Heat a medium-sized non-stick pan over medium heat, and coat with olive oil spray.

2. Next, add the turkey bacon, cook until brown, flip, and cook for 5 to 6 minutes. Remove and rest on a cutting board, allowing it to cool. Crumble the cooled turkey bacon by hand or coarsely chop.

3. Place the spinach on a large serving platter. Then arrange the mushroom, carrot, cucumber, kidney beans, avocado, blue cheese, and turkey bacon in neat rows atop the spinach.

4. Serve with vinaigrette on the side to enjoy.

Nutritional value

Calories: 232 kcal | Carbohydrates: 19g | Protein: 11g | Total Fat: 14g | Sugar: 1g | Cholesterol: 23 mg | Sodium: 612mg | Dietary

Fiber: 9g | Saturated Fat: 4 | Potassium: 797 mg | Calcium: 13%|

Fiber: 2g | Saturated Fat: 3 | Potassium: 643mg | Calcium: 9%|

Beet & Heirloom Tomato Salad

Preparation Time: 20 min
Cooking Time: 15 min| Servings: 4

Ingredients

1 cup cooked, thinly sliced beets

¼ cup toasted walnut pieces

¼ cup crumbled goat cheese

6 cups mixed greens

1 cup green heirloom tomato, sliced and cut in fourths

¼ cup balsamic vinegar

Cracked black pepper, to taste

Preparation

1. Prepare the beets by cutting off the green stems and washing them beets. Cut off the very top and very bottom of the beet, and then peel off the thick skin.
2. Place the beets in a small pot with about ½ to 1 cup of water and steam over medium heat for about 15 minutes.
3. Once cooked, allow to cool, and then slice and cut each slice into fourths as with the heirloom tomatoes.
4. Put the mixed greens in a large salad bowl and top with the beets, tomato, walnuts, and goat cheese.
5. Drizzle with balsamic vinegar, and grind cracked black pepper over the top to enjoy.

Nutritional value

Calories: 168kcal | Carbohydrates: 156g |Protein: 8g |Total Fat: 10g |Sugar: 6g | Cholesterol: 11mg | Sodium: 257mg |Dietary

Mixed Bean Salad

Preparation Time: 5 min
Cooking Time: 5 min | Servings: 8

Ingredients

¼ cup orange juice

1 can unsalted kidney beans

½ cup vinegar

1 can of low-sodium green beans

1 can of low-sodium wax beans

¼ cup onion

1 can garbanzo beans

Sugar (optional)

Preparation

1. Get your favorite salad bowl and mix the kidney beans, green beans, garbanzo beans, wax beans, and onion. Ensure to toss well so that they all mix evenly.
2. While in another separate bowl, mix sugar, orange juice, and vinegar and add over the bean mixture. Mix well and refrigerate before serving.

Nutritional value

Calories: 289 kcal | Carbohydrates: 50g |Protein: 6g |Total Fat: 5g | Total Sugar: 4g | Cholesterol: 7mg | Sodium: 808mg |Dietary Fiber: 14g | Saturated Fat: 1g|

Potato Salad

Preparation Time: 10 min
Cooking Time: 10 min | Servings: 8

Ingredients

1 pound of potatoes, diced and boiled or steamed

1 large yellow onion, chopped (1 cup)

1 large carrot, diced (½ cup)

2 ribs celery, diced (½ cup)

1 tbsp Dijon mustard

2 tbsp red wine vinegar

2 tbsps minced fresh dill (or 1/2 tablespoon dried)

1 tsp ground black pepper

¼ cup low-calorie mayonnaise

Preparation

1. Mix all ingredients carefully in a bowl.
2. Chill before serving to enjoy.

Nutritional value

Calories: 77kcal | Carbohydrates: 14g |Protein: 1g |Total Fat: 1g |Total Sugar: 2g | Cholesterol: 2mg | Sodium: 127mg |Dietary Fiber: 2g | Saturated Fat: Trace |

Cucumber Pineapple Salad

Preparation Time: 15 min

Cooking Time: 15 min | Servings: 4

Ingredients

¼ cup sugar

⅓ cup thinly sliced red onion

4 cups torn salad greens

1 tbsp sesame seeds, toasted

⅔ cup rice wine vinegar

2 tablespoons water

1 cup canned, no-sugar-added pineapple chunks

1 cucumber, thinly sliced

1 carrot, cut into thin strips

Preparation

1. Bring the sugar, vinegar, and water to a boil in a saucepan. Stir until reduced to about ½ cup, for 5 minutes.

2. Transfer to a large bowl and place in the refrigerator until cool. Add the pineapple, cucumber, carrot, and red onion to the mixture. Toss well.

3. To serve, divide the salad greens among individual plates. Top with the pineapple mixture and sprinkle with toasted sesame seeds.

4. Serve immediately to enjoy.

Nutritional value

Calories: 129 kcal | Carbohydrates: 28g |Protein: 2g |Total Fat: 1g |Total Sugar: 23g | Cholesterol: 0mg | Sodium: 102mg |Dietary Fiber: 2g | Saturated Fat: Trace |

Tuna Salad

Preparation Time: 10 min

Cooking Time: 10 min | Servings: 4

Ingredients

¼ cup chopped celery

½ jalapeño chile pepper, seeded and chopped

¼ cup chopped Roma tomato

3 tbsps low-fat plain Greek yogurt

⅛ tsp cracked black pepper

1 small avocado, thinly sliced

¼ cup chopped red onion

2 (6-ounce) cans of albacore tuna in water, no salt added, drained

1 tsp brown mustard

Preparation

1. Combine the celery, chile pepper, tomato, and onion in a medium bowl. Mix in the tuna, mustard, yogurt, and pepper until well combined.

2. Top the salad with avocado slices, and serve to enjoy.

Nutritional value

Calories: 162kcal | Carbohydrates: 32g |Protein: 21g |Total Fat: 7g |Sugar: 1g | Cholesterol: 38mg | Sodium: 241mg |Dietary Fiber: 6g | Saturated Fat: 0.9 | Potassium: 318mg | Calcium: 4%|

Pickled Onion Salad

Preparation Time: 1 hr 20 min

Cooking Time: 1 hr 20 min | Servings: 8

Ingredients

4 lettuce leaves

2 large red onions, thinly sliced (about 2 cups)

4 spring (green) onions with tops, chopped

½ cup cider vinegar

2 tsp olive oil

2 tbsps sugar

½ cup fresh cilantro, chopped

1 tbsp lime juice

Preparation

1. Combine the onions, vinegar, oil, and sugar in a small bowl. Stir to mix evenly.
2. Cover and refrigerate until well chilled for about 60 minutes. Before serving, stir in the cilantro and sprinkle with lime juice.
3. Serve mounded on a leaf of lettuce to enjoy.

Nutritional value

Calories: 86kcal | Carbohydrates: 16g |Protein: 1g |Total Fat: 2g |Sugar: 12g | Cholesterol: 0mg | Sodium: 21mg |Dietary Fiber: 2g | Saturated Fat: Trace |

Taco Chicken Salad

Preparation Time: 10 min

Cooking Time: 10 min | Servings: 1

Ingredients

4 mini taco shells or scoop-shaped tortilla chips

⅓ cup chopped or shredded cooked chicken or low-sodium turkey

2 tbsps chopped celery

1 tbsp light mayonnaise dressing or salad dressing

1 tbsp salsa

1 tbsp shredded cheddar cheese

Preparation

1. For chicken salad, combine chicken, celery, mayonnaise dressing, salsa, and cheese in a small bowl and toss to mix.
2. Spoon the salad into a container and cover it tightly. Wrap taco shells in plastic wrap and pack a chicken salad and taco shells into an insulated bag with an ice pack.
3. When serving, use the taco shells to scoop up the salad.

Nutritional value

Calories: 510kcal | Carbohydrates: 45g |Protein: 27g |Total Fat: 26g |Sugar: 7g | Cholesterol: 80mg | Sodium: 650mg |Dietary Fiber: 8g | Saturated Fat: 10g |

Yellow Pear and Cherry Tomato Salad

Preparation Time: 20 min

Cooking Time: 10 min | Servings: 6

Ingredients

For the vinaigrette

2 tbsps sherry vinegar or red wine vinegar

1 tsp minced shallot

1 tsp extra-virgin olive oil

¼ tsp salt

4 large fresh basil leaves, cut into slender ribbons

1/8 teaspoon freshly ground black pepper

1 ½ cups yellow pear tomatoes, halved

1 ½ cups orange cherry tomatoes, halved

1 ½ cups red cherry tomatoes, halved

Preparation

1. To make the vinaigrette, combine the vinegar and shallot in a small bowl and let stand for 15 minutes.
2. Add the olive oil, salt, and pepper and whisk until well blended.
3. In a large serving or salad bowl, toss together all the tomatoes.
4. Pour the vinaigrette over the tomatoes, add the basil shreds, and toss gently to mix well and coat evenly.
5. Serve immediately to enjoy.

Nutritional value

Calories: 47kcal | Carbohydrates: 4g |Protein: 1g |Total Fat: 3g |Sugar: 0g | Cholesterol: 0mg | Sodium: 125mg |Dietary Fiber: 1g | Saturated Fat: 0g | Potassium: 405mg|

Spiced Melon Salad

Preparation Time: 10 min

Cooking Time: 10 min | Servings: 4

Ingredients

½ cup plain or vanilla low-fat or non-fat yogurt

2 cups diced assorted melon, such as cantaloupe, honeydew, or watermelon (or any fruit of choice)

¼ tsp nutmeg

¼ tsp mace

⅛ tsp clove

⅛ tsp cinnamon

Orange zest (about 1 tbsp) and juice (about 3 tbsps)

Preparation

1. In a large bowl, mix all ingredients to combine.
2. Serve to enjoy.

Nutritional value

Calories: 52kcal | Carbohydrates: 11g |Protein: 2g |Total Fat: Trace |Sugar: 0g | Cholesterol: 1mg | Sodium: 31mg |Dietary Fiber: 1g | Saturated Fat: Trace |

Apple-Fennel Slaw

Preparation Time: 15 min

Cooking Time: 20 min | Servings: 4

Ingredients

½ cup apple juice

2 tbsps apple cider vinegar

1 medium-sized fennel bulb

1 large apple, thinly sliced

2 carrots

4 lettuce leaves

2 tbsps raisins

1 tbsp olive oil

1 tsp sugar

Preparation

1. Combine the fennel, apple, carrots, and raisins in your salad bowl. Add olive oil, and cover to refrigerate.
2. Meanwhile, to make the dressing, mix the sugar and apple juice in a small saucepan and cook on medium heat. Once ready, remove from the heat and allow to cool.
3. Add in the apple cider vinegar and pour the apple juice mixture over the salad toss to combine. Serve chilled to enjoy.

Nutritional value

Calories: 128kcal | Carbohydrates: 22g |Protein: 2g |Total Fat: 9mg |Sugar: 1g | Cholesterol: 0mg | Sodium: 204mg |Dietary Fiber: 4g | Saturated Fat: 1mg |

Caprese Salad with Balsamic Glaze

Preparation Time: 10 min

Cooking Time: 2 min | Servings: 8

Ingredients

1 pound fresh buffalo mozzarella cheese

5 large beefsteak tomatoes

1 bunch of fresh basil

⅛ tsp cracked black pepper

5 tbsps Balsamic Glaze

5 tbsps olive oil

Pinch of sea salt

Preparation

1. Slice your tomatoes into ½ inch slices. On a large platter, arrange the sliced tomatoes and top each piece with a large basil leaf and a mozzarella slice.
2. Drizzle balsamic glaze and oil over the platter, then sprinkle with salt and pepper.

Nutritional value

Calories: 334 kcal | Carbohydrates: 11g |Protein: 19g |Total Fat: 24| Added Sugar: 4g | Cholesterol: 43mg | Sodium: 10mg |Dietary Fiber: 2g | Saturated Fat: 9|

Butternut Squash and Apple Salad

Preparation Time: 20 min

Cooking Time: 30 min | Servings: 6

Ingredients

2 cups carrots, chopped

1 butternut squash

6 cups arugula, chopped

2 tbsp olive oil

2 large apples, cut into pieces

6 cups spinach, chopped

1 ½ cups chopped celery

2 tbsp balsamic vinegar

1 ½ tsp honey

½ cup low-fat plain yogurt

Preparation

1. Place the squash in olive oil and roast in the preheated 400°F oven for 20 - 30 minutes. Once soft and golden browned, remove and cool completely, then combine all vegetables in a large bowl.
2. Mix the yogurt, vinegar, and honey for the dressing until smooth.
3. Pour dressing over the salad. Toss and enjoy.

Nutritional value

Calories: 205kcal | Carbohydrates: 35g |Protein: 4g |Total Fat: 7g | Added Sugar: 22g | Cholesterol: 0mg | Sodium: 632mg |Dietary Fiber: 7g | Saturated Fat: 1g |

Mexican Summer Salad

Preparation Time: 10 min

Cooking Time: 10 min | Servings: 6

Ingredients

1 ½ cups sliced unpeeled cucumber

¼ cup very thinly sliced white onion

3 heads romaine lettuce, chopped

5 Roma tomatoes, chopped

¼ cup fresh lime juice

⅛ cup extra virgin olive oil

Sea salt

Cracked black pepper

Preparation

1. Combine the lettuce, tomato, cucumber, and onion in a large bowl. Pour the lime juice and oil over the salad, and toss well.

2. Season to taste with salt and pepper. Serve to enjoy.

Nutritional value

Calories: 78 kcal | Carbohydrates: 9g |Protein: 1g |Total Fat: 5g |Sugar: 0.2g | Cholesterol: 0mg | Sodium: 61mg |Dietary Fiber: 2g | Saturated Fat: 0.7g | Potassium: 405mg|

Italian Style Tuna Salad

Preparation Time: 10 min

Cooking Time: 10 min | Servings: 6

Ingredients

2 cans of albacore tuna

½ cup chopped Roma tomato

Juice of 1 lemon

4 tbsps extra virgin olive oil

1/4 cup chopped red onion

4 tbsps finely chopped fresh parsley

⅛ tsp cracked black pepper

Preparation

1. Put all the ingredients in a large bowl, and stir to incorporate evenly.

2. Let sit for 30 minutes before serving.

Nutritional value

Calories: 205kcal | Carbohydrates: 4g |Protein: 19g |Total Fat: 15g |Sugar: 2g | Cholesterol: 38mg | Sodium: 192mg |Dietary Fiber: 2g | Saturated Fat: 0.7g | Potassium: 94mg|

Italian Tortellini Salad

Preparation Time: 20 min

Cooking Time: 2 hrs 30 min | Servings: 8

Ingredients

1 pound light cheese tortellini or ravioli

1 cup sliced carrots (2 medium)

¼ cup sliced green onions

½ cup bottled reduced-fat ranch salad dressing

3 cups broccoli florets

1 large tomato, chopped

1 cup fresh pea pods

Milk (optional)

Preparation

1. Boil the pasta in a large saucepan. Add the sliced carrots and broccoli when almost boiled.

2. Drain, and rinse the cooked pasta and vegetables with cold water. Combine the cooked pasta mix and green onions in a large bowl, drizzle with dressing, and gently toss to coat.

3. Cover and chill for 2 hours. Gently stir the tomato and pea pods into the pasta mix before serving. Stir in a little milk to moisten if necessary.

Nutritional value

Calories: 304 kcal | Carbohydrates: 30g |Protein: 12g |Total Fat: 15g |Sugar: 6g | Cholesterol: 31mg | Sodium: 800mg |Dietary Fiber: 3g | Saturated Fat: 4g | Potassium: 94mg|

Avocado, Strawberry & Melon Salad

Preparation Time: 15 min

Cooking Time: 15 min | Servings: 2

Ingredients

1 small avocado

¼ cup honey

2 tbsps red wine vinegar

2 tbsps finely chopped fresh mint

¼ tsp freshly ground pepper

Pinch of salt

4 cups baby spinach

½ small cantaloupe

Strawberries, sliced

2 tsp sesame seeds, toasted

Preparation

1. Mix honey, vinegar, fresh mint, pepper, and salt in a small bowl. Divide the baby spinach equally onto a serving plate.

2. Arrange the slices of avocado and cantaloupe in a fan on top of the spinach alternatively. Top each salad with strawberries and drizzle it with the honey dressing. Sprinkle sesame seeds on top and serve.

Nutritional value

Calories: 610 kcal | Carbohydrates: 44g |Protein: 6g |Total Fat: 50g |Sugar: 30g | Cholesterol: 38mg | Sodium: 23mg |Dietary Fiber: 12g | Saturated Fat: 6g |

Quinoa Salad

Preparation Time: 15 min

Coking Time: 20 min | Servings: 4

Ingredients

11 cups quinoa

2 cups water

1/4 cup sliced almonds

1/4 cup crumbled feta cheese

1/4 cup chopped sun-dried tomatoes

1/4 cup chopped olives

2 tsp chopped fresh parsley

2 tsp lemon juice

2 tsp olive oil

Salt and black pepper to taste

Preparation

1. Rinse quinoa and add to a medium-sized pot with water. Then, bring the water to a boil, and decrease the heat to low.

2. Simmer for 20 minutes or until the water is absorbed and the quinoa is tender.

3. Preheat the oven to 350°F. Spread the sliced almonds on a baking sheet and toast in the oven for 8-10 minutes or until golden brown.

4. Combine the cooked quinoa, toasted almonds, feta cheese, sun-dried tomatoes, olives, and parsley in a large bowl.

5. Whisk the lemon juice, olive oil, salt, and black pepper in a small bowl.

6. Pour the dressing over the quinoa and mix.

7. Serve and enjoy!

Nutritional value

Calories: 250 kcal | Carbohydrates: 30g |Protein: 8g |Total Fat: 11g |Sugar: 3g | Cholesterol: 0mg | Sodium: 40mg |Dietary Fiber: 6g | Saturated Fat: 2g |

DASH Diet Fish and Seafood

In this section, you'll find low-salt fish and seafood recipes for lowering blood pressure, losing weight, and improving your health. Enjoy.

Fish Veracruz

Preparation Time: 10 min

Cooking Time: 50 min | Servings: 4

Ingredients

½ cup low-sodium tomato sauce

2 pounds of whitefish fillets

4 tbsps fresh cilantro, chopped

1 lime cut into 8 wedges

1 small onion, chopped

1 small green bell pepper, chopped

¼ cup lime juice

½ tbsps olive oil

¼ cup jalapeno pepper, chopped

½ cup olives, sliced

1 tbsp capers

2 cups fresh salsa

Preparation

1. Place fish in a baking pan and sprinkle with lime juice, salt, and pepper. Allow marinating for 20 minutes. Meanwhile, preheat oven to 425°F.

2. In a large pan, heat the oil on medium heat. Add onion, bell pepper, and jalapeno pepper. Stir until vegetables are tender.

3. Stir in salsa, tomato sauce, olives, and capers. Cover to cook on medium heat for 10 minutes.

4. Pour the sauce over the fish and bake for 20 minutes until done. Serve with cilantro and lime wedges to enjoy.

Nutritional value

Calories: 907kcal | Carbohydrates: 20g |Protein: 7|Total Fat: 83g |Sugar: 11g |

Cholesterol: 57mg | Sodium: 160mg |Dietary Fiber: 6g | Saturated Fat: 6g |

Tortilla-Crusted Salmon with Salsa

Preparation Time: 15 min

Cooking Time: 30 min | Servings: 4

Ingredients

4 salmon fillets

Salt and freshly ground black pepper

½ cup fresh pineapple, diced

2 tbsps red or white onion

2 tbsps. fresh lime juice

1 tbsp Dijon mustard

4 cups corn tortilla chips

1 mango, diced

1 papaya, diced

2 tbsps. chopped fresh cilantro

Preparation

1. Preheat the oven to 400°F. Add salt and pepper to the salmon for proper seasoning. Rub the mustard on top of the salmon. Crush the chips into tiny crumbs and place them in a dish.

2. Place the seasoned salmon in the dish with the side with mustard touching the chips. Allow the chips to coat the salmon well, and place the salmon in the baking tray.

3. Bake for about 15 minutes until the pieces of the fish come apart.

4. Mix mango, pineapple, onion, papaya, lime juice, and cilantro to make the salsa.

5. Adjust seasonings with salt and pepper.
6. Spread the salsa on top of the salmon and serve.

Nutritional value

Calories: 1045 kcal | Carbohydrates: 106g |Protein: 58g |Total Fat: 45g |Sugar: 14g | Cholesterol: 335 mg | Sodium: 1549 mg |Dietary Fiber: 11g | Saturated Fat: 9g |

Asian Grilled Salmon

Preparation Time: 5 min
Cooking Time: 60 min | Servings: 4

Ingredients

1 tbsp fresh ginger, minced

1 tbsp rice wine vinegar

4 salmon fillets

1 tbsp olive oil

1 tbsp low-sodium soy sauce

Preparation

1. Add sesame oil, soy sauce, ginger, and vinegar to a dish and combine gently. Add the salmon and gently coat all sides. Leave in the refrigerator to marinate for 60 minutes.
2. Oil your grill and heat on medium-high heat. Gently place the salmon on the grill and grill for 5 minutes on each side.
3. Transfer to a plate and serve warm to enjoy.

Nutritional value

Calories: 599kcal | Carbohydrates: 1g |Protein: 47g |Total Fat: 44g |Sugar: 0g | Cholesterol: 125mg | Sodium: 631mg |Dietary Fiber: 0g| Saturated Fat: 9g |

Chipotle Spiced Shrimp

Preparation Time: 20 min
Cooking Time: 10 min| Servings: 4

Ingredients

1 pound uncooked shrimp, peeled and deveined

½ tsp chipotle chili powder

½ tsp chopped fresh oregano

2 tbsps tomato paste

1 ½ tsp water

½ tsp extra-virgin olive oil

½ tsp minced garlic

Preparation

1. Rinse the shrimp in cold water and dry them with a paper towel.
2. Whisk the tomato paste, water, and oil in a small bowl. Add garlic, chili powder, and oregano. Mix well.
3. Spread the marinade on both sides of the shrimp using a brush and place it in the refrigerator.
4. Heat a grill or broiler. Away from the heat source, lightly coat the grill rack or broiler pan with cooking spray.
5. Put the shrimp in a grill basket or on skewers and place them on the grill. Turn the shrimp after 3 to 4 minutes. The cooking time varies depending on the heat of the fire, so observe.
6. Transfer to a plate and serve immediately to enjoy.

Nutritional value

Calories: 109kcal | Carbohydrates: 2g |Protein: 23g |Total Fat: 1g |Sugar: 0g | Cholesterol: 182mg | Sodium: 139mg |Dietary Fiber: 0.5g |

Tacos with Cilantro - Lime- Tilapia

Preparation Time: 5 min
Cooking Time: 10 min | Servings: 4

Ingredients

1 pound tilapia filets, rinsed and patted dry

1 tsp olive oil

1 small onion, chopped

2 cups diced tomatoes

¼ cup fresh cilantro, chopped

4 cloves garlic, finely minced

2 jalapeno peppers, chopped (seeds removed for less heat)

3 tbsps lime juice

Preparation

1. Heat olive oil in a skillet. Saute onions until translucent, then add garlic. Mix well. Place tilapia in the skillet and cook until the flesh starts to flake.

2. Add jalapeno peppers, tomatoes, cilantro, and lime juice. Saute over medium-high heat for about 5 minutes, breaking up the fish to get everything mixed well.

3. Season to taste with a bit of cracked pepper. Meanwhile, heat tortillas on a skillet for a few minutes on each side to warm.

4. Serve a little over ¼ cup of fish on each warmed tortilla with two slices of avocado.

5. Split ¼ cup of shredded cabbage and 1 tbsp of low-fat or fat-free sour cream (optional) between 2 tacos.

6. Garnish with fresh chopped cilantro and lime wedges.

Nutritional value

Calories: 427 kcal | Carbohydrates: 45g |Protein: 35g |Total Fat: 12g |Sugar: 0g | Calcium: 60mg | Sodium: 142mg |Dietary Fiber: 5mg | Saturated Fat: 2g |

Spicy Sole and Vegetables

Preparation Time: 10 min

Cooking Time: 15 min | Servings: 1

Ingredients

4 sole fillets (4 ounces each)

2 tbsps butter

2 cups sliced fresh mushrooms

2 garlic cloves, minced

½ cup of finely chopped bell peppers

2 green onions, thinly sliced

¼ tsp paprika

¼ tsp lemon-pepper seasoning

⅛ tsp cayenne pepper

1 medium tomato, chopped

Preparation

1. In a large skillet, heat butter on medium-high heat. Add bell peppers and mushrooms; cook and stir until tender. Then, add garlic and cook 1 minute longer.

2. Place fillets over mushrooms. Sprinkle with paprika, lemon pepper, and cayenne.

3. Cook while covered on medium heat for 5-10 minutes.

4. Sprinkle with tomato and green onions to enjoy.

Nutritional value

Calories: 174kcal | Carbohydrates: 4g |Protein: 23g |Total Fat: 7g |Sugar: 2g | Calcium: 60mg | Sodium: 136mg |Dietary Fiber: 1mg | Saturated Fat: 4g | Cholesterol: 69mg |

Lemon Baked Fish

Preparation Time: 15 min

Cooking Time: 25 min | Servings: 1

Ingredient

4 cod fillets

¼ cup flour

3 tbsps lemon juice

4 garlic cloves, crushed

2 tbsps minced fresh parsley

2 tbsps grated lemon rind

3 tbsps butter, melted

¼ tsp paprika

¼ tsp lemon-pepper seasoning

Preparation

1. Preheat the oven to 400°F. Combine the lemon juice, garlic, and butter in a saucepan and cook for 3 minutes until fragrant.

2. In a separate bowl, mix flour and seasonings. Place the fillets in the lemon juice mixture, then in the flour mixture, coating both sides.

3. Put the fish in the baking pan and drizzle with the remaining lemon juice mixture. Bake for 12-15 minutes or until cooked.

4. Mix parsley and lemon peel and sprinkle over fish to enjoy.

Nutritional value

Calories: 275 kcal | Carbohydrates: 7g |Protein: 40g |Total Fat: 10g |Sugar: 0g | Calcium: 28mg | Sodium: 180mg |Dietary Fiber: 0mg | Saturated Fat: 6g | Cholesterol: 122mg |

Pesto Salmon

Preparation Time: 10 min

Cooking Time: 20 min | Servings: 4

Ingredients

4 pounds of salmon fillets

½ tsp ground black pepper

½ tsp kosher salt

1 tbsp toasted and chopped pine nuts

2 lemons

3 tbsp pesto

Olive oil

Preparation

1. Preheat the oven to 325°F. Stir 4 cups of water and 3 tbsps kosher salt in a bowl. Place the salmon in the water and allow it to sit for 15 minutes.

2. Lightly oil a baking pan with olive oil and place salmon in. Sprinkle the salmon with kosher salt and fresh ground pepper and allow to bake for 10 minutes.

3. Once done, remove the salmon and spread pesto over the salmon. Sprinkle with chopped pine nuts and lemon zest (optional)to enjoy.

Nutritional value

Calories: 272kcal | Carbohydrates: 0.7g |Protein: 63g |Total Fat: 67g |Sugar: 0g | Calcium: 35.1mg | Sodium: 851mg |Dietary Fiber: 0mg | Saturated Fat: 16g| Potassium: 1195mg|

Garlic Butter Shrimp

Preparation Time: 10 min

Cooking Time: 10 min| Servings: 4

Ingredients

1 pound medium shrimp

3 garlic cloves, crushed

½ tsp kosher salt

3 tbsps unsalted butter

2 lemon wedges

Freshly ground black pepper

Fresh cilantro or parsley leaves

Preparation

1. Mix the shrimp with garlic, salt, and pepper in a medium bowl.

2. Melt butter in a large skillet on medium-high heat and cook the shrimp for 1 to 2 minutes per side until cooked. Gently toss to combine.

3. Squeeze lemon juice and serve immediately to enjoy.

Nutritional value

Calories: 272 kcal | Carbohydrates: 8g |Protein: 23g |Total Fat: 12g |Sugar: 0g | Calcium: 79.3mg | Sodium: 477mg |Dietary Fiber: 2mg | Saturated Fat: 7g| Potassium: 161 mg|

Roasted Salmon

Preparation Time: 15 min

Cooking Time: 15 min | Servings: 2

Ingredients

Two 5-ounce pieces of salmon with skin

2 tbsps extra-virgin olive oil

1 tsp chopped chives

1 tsp fresh tarragon leaves (optional)

Preparation

1. Heat the oven to 425°F. Cover a baking sheet with foil.

2. Rub salmon all over with 2 teaspoons oil. Roast skin on a foil-lined baking sheet until fish is cooked through, about 12 minutes. After 10 minutes, check if the fish flakes easily with a fork. Suppose it doesn't; continue baking for 2 more minutes.

3. Using a metal spatula, lift the salmon off the skin and place the salmon on a serving plate. Discard skin. Sprinkle salmon with herbs and serve.

Nutritional value

Calories: 244 kcal | Carbohydrates: Trace |Protein: 28g |Total Fat: 14g |Sugar: 0g |

Calcium: 35.1mg | Sodium: 63mg |Dietary Fiber: Trace | Saturated Fat: 2g| Potassium: 723 mg| Cholesterol: 78mg |

Salmon Salad in a Pita

Preparation Time: 10 min

Cooking Time: 10 min | Servings: 1

Ingredient

3⁄4 cup canned salmon

3 tbsps plain fat-free yogurt

1 tbsp lemon juice

3 lettuce leaves

2 tbsps red bell pepper, minced

1 tbsp red onion, minced

1 tsp capers, rinsed and chopped

Fresh or dried dill

Black pepper to taste

Preparation

1. Mix the salmon, fat-free yogurt, lemon juice, red bell pepper, red onion, capers, dill, and black pepper to make the salmon salad.

2. Place a lettuce leaf and ⅓ cup of the salmon salad inside each pita to enjoy.

Nutritional value

Calories: 239 kcal | Carbohydrates: 19 |Protein: 25g |Total Fat: 7g |Sugar: 3g | Calcium: 35.1mg |Sodium: 510mg |Dietary Fiber: 2mg | Saturated Fat: 1g|Cholesterol: 68mg |

Shrimps Kebab

Preparation Time: 10 min

Cooking Time: 5 min | Servings: 2

Ingredients

12 pieces shrimp, peeled and deveined

2 wooden skewers (8 inches each)

1 lemon, juiced

2 tsp finely minced garlic

1 tsp finely chopped fresh tarragon

1 tsp finely chopped fresh rosemary

1 tbsp olive oil

½ tsp kosher salt

¼ tsp ground black pepper

Preparation

1. Soak skewers in water for 10 minutes and preheat the grill to high.

2. Combine lemon juice, olive oil, garlic, herbs, and seasonings in a medium glass bowl. Place shrimp into the lemon marinade and allow to stand for 5 minutes. Skewer the shrimp and place them on the grill.

3. Cook for 2 minutes on every side or until the shrimp is thoroughly cooked.

4. Serve to enjoy.

Nutritional value

Calories: 105kcal | Carbohydrates: 0mg |Protein: 24g |Total Fat: 1g |Sugar: 0g | Calcium: 35.1mg | Sodium: 185mg |Dietary Fiber: 0mg | Saturated Fat: 0mg|Cholesterol: 180mg |

Lemon Dill Salmon

Preparation Time: 10 min

Cooking Time: 25 min | Servings: 4

Ingredients

4 salmon fillets

1 tsp lemon juice

2 tbsps dill, chopped

¼ tsp onion powder

¼ cup Greek yogurt

6 tbsps mayonnaise

Black pepper

¼ tsp garlic powder

⅛ tsp kosher salt

2 tsps water

Preparation

1. Preheat the oven to 450°F and lightly grease a baking pan. Sprinkle salmon with kosher salt, dill, garlic and garlic powder, and black pepper, and place on a baking sheet to bake for about 10 minutes until cooked.

2. Mix water, lemon juice, mayonnaise, and yogurt, in a small bowl to drizzle over the salmon.

3. Serve and garnish with lemon dill sauce.

Nutritional value

Calories: 313kcal | Carbohydrates: 2g |Protein: 26g |Total Fat: 22g |Sugar: 0.9g | Calcium: 58.2mg | Sodium: 197mg |Dietary Fiber:0mg | Saturated Fat: 9g| Cholesterol: 49mg |

Snapper with Citrus Salsa

Preparation Time: 20 min

Cooking Time: 40 min | Servings: 4

Ingredients

2 red snapper fillets

2 ounces baby spinach (about 2 cups)

1 large navel orange

½ medium lemon

½ small shallot, thinly sliced

¼ tsp of red chile flakes

1 tbsp coarsely chopped fresh cilantro

Zest 1/2 lime, plus 1 tablespoon of fresh lime juice

1 tbsp extra-virgin olive oil

¼ tsp freshly ground pepper

Preparation

1. Toss oranges, lemon, shallot, chili, cilantro, lime zest and juice, oil, honey, and ⅛ tsp each salt and pepper in a bowl. Stay at room temperature for 15 minutes, gently stirring occasionally.

2. Fill a wok or large pot with 1 inch of water. Bring to a boil. Line the bottom of the basket of a round bamboo steamer with parchment paper. (Or use two pots fitted with steamer inserts).

3. Season fish using the remaining pepper. Arrange in a single layer in the bottom basket. Cover, and set over boiling water. Steam until fish is almost cooked through, about 5 minutes.

4. Put the spinach into the top basket, and set it over the bottom basket. Steam until spinach is bright green and wilted, about 2 minutes more.

5. Divide spinach among 2 plates. Top each with fish and ½ cup salsa. Serve the remaining salsa on the side.

Nutritional value

Calories: 164kcal | Carbohydrates: 3g |Protein: 32g |Total Fat: 7g |Sugar: 0g | Calcium: 4% | Sodium: 628mg |Dietary Fiber: 1mg | Saturated Fat: 1g| Cholesterol: 26mg |

Pan Fried Cod

Preparation Time: 10 min

Cooking Time: 15 min| Servings: 4

Ingredients

2 pounds of cod fillets

1 tbsp unsalted butter

½ tsp onion powder

⅛ tsp celery seed

1 tbsp lemon juice

2 tsp smoked paprika

½ tsp garlic powder

2 tbsps parsley, chopped

1 tsp kosher salt

2 tbsps olive oil

Preparation

1. Mix the smoked paprika, onion and garlic powder, celery seed, and kosher salt in a large bowl. Pat the cod dry and season both sides with salt and pepper.

2. In medium-high heat, heat a saucepan, adding butter and olive oil. Once the butter is melted, add the cod and cook for 2 minutes.

3. Gently flip the cod and sprinkle it with lemon juice. Cook for an additional 2 minutes until the cod is tender.

4. Once done, remove from heat and sprinkle with the parsley to enjoy.

Nutritional value

Calories: 221 kcal | Carbohydrates: 0.8g |Protein: 31g |Total Fat: 21g |Sugar: 1g | Calcium: 42.7mg |Dietary Fiber: 0.1mg | Saturated Fat: 2.9mg|Cholesterol: 88mg |Potassium: 799mg |

Sole Stuffed With Spinach

Preparation Time: 20 min

Cooking Time: 20 min | Servings: 4

Ingredients

2 sole fillets

1 tsp olive oil

½ tsp butter

2 tsp garlic, minced

2 cups fresh spinach leaves

Ground black pepper

Preparation

1. Firstly, if you are using fresh spinach, blanch before use, and if frozen, thaw before use. Ensure to drain out any excess liquid and chop to the desired size. Meanwhile, heat your oven to 400°F and spray your baking dish sparingly.

2. Get a large skillet and saute the spinach, garlic, and pepper in olive oil for 3 minutes. Place the sole fillets in the baking dish with a portion of the spinach mixture in the middle of each fillet and roll up from one end to the other.

3. Continue until you have successfully stuffed all fillets, then coat them with melted butter. Bake for 10 minutes until cooked thoroughly.

Nutritional value

Calories: 208kcal | Carbohydrates: 10.8g |Protein: 28g |Total Fat: 2.8g |Sugar: 8g | Calcium: 35.1mg | Sodium: 242.8mg |Dietary Fiber: 1mg | Saturated Fat: 1mg|Cholesterol: 78.2mg |

Sweet Pepper Fish Salsa

Preparation Time: 10 min
Cooking Time: 10 min | Servings: 4

Ingredients

1 pound fresh skinless fish fillets

2 tbsps olive oil

1½ cups fresh mushrooms

1 cup green or yellow sweet pepper

1 small onion, chopped

1 cup salsa

Fresh oregano (optional)

Preparation

1. Prep the fish by dividing the fillets into 4 portions. Rinse the fish well with cold water, pat dry, and set aside.

2. Heat a tbsp of cooking oil in a large skillet. Add the green or yellow sweet pepper, mushrooms, and onion to the skillet and cook until soft.

3. Take off the vegetables from the skillet and set aside. Add the remaining cooking oil to the skillet, heat, and add the fish fillets.

4. Cook the fish over medium heat until it starts to flake. Place the cooked vegetables and salsa over the fish, cover, and cook on a low heat setting until heated through.

5. Serve the fish fillets and garnish each dish with oregano if desired.

Nutritional value

Calories: 213kcal | Carbohydrates: 13g |Protein: 22g |Total Fat: 8g |Sugar: 10mg | Sodium: 686mg |Dietary Fiber: 2g| Saturated Fat: 1mg|Cholesterol: 77mg |

Low-Carb White Sea Bass with Dill Relish

Preparation Time: 10 min
Cooking Time: 15 min | Servings: 4

Ingredients

2 tsps baby pickled capers

4 white sea bass fillets

1 tsp Dijon mustard

1 tsp lemon juice

1 white onion, chopped

1 ½ tsp dill, chopped

1 lemon

Preparation

1. Add the onion, capers, dill, mustard, and lemon juice in a small bowl, and combine thoroughly to ensure they mix evenly. Meanwhile, set your oven to 375°F.

2. Place each fillet on an aluminum foil. Get your fresh lemon wedge and drizzle over each fillet. Also, spread equal portions of the dill relish on each fillet.

3. Gently wrap the foil around the fish and bake for 12 minutes until the fish is cooked through. Serve immediately.

Nutritional value

Calories: 133.3kcal | Carbohydrates: 3.5g |Protein: 24.2g |Total Fat: 2.65g |Sugar: 0.64g | Sodium: 127mg |Dietary Fiber: 1.4g | Saturated Fat: 1mg|Cholesterol: 46mg |

Shrimp and Broccoli

Preparation Time: 20 min

Cooking Time: 15 min | Servings: 4

Ingredients

1 pound large shrimp

1 ½ pounds broccoli florets

4 tbsps soy sauce

½ tbsp chili garlic sauce

2 tbsps sesame oil

1 onion

2 tbsps rice vinegar

¼ tsp kosher salt

Green onion, for garnish

Preparation

1. Heat the sesame oil in a skillet on medium-high heat. Chop the broccoli, add the chopped pieces, onion, and kosher salt, and cook for 5 to 6 minutes until tender.

2. Meanwhile, whisk together rice vinegar, soy sauce, and chili garlic sauce.

3. Place the shrimp in the skillet and cook for 3 - 4 minutes.

4. Once done, add the sauce mixture and cook for 1 minute until thickened. Garnish with green onion to enjoy.

Nutritional value

Calories: 214 kcal | Carbohydrates: 17.2g |Protein: 21g |Total Fat: 9g |Sugar: 2mg | Sodium: 287 mg |Dietary Fiber: 2g| Cholesterol: 183 mg | Calcium: 159 mg

Lemon Tilapia

Preparation Time: 15 min

Cooking Time: 20-25 min | Servings: 4

Ingredients

4 tilapia fillets (6 oz. each)

¼ cup all-purpose flour

¼ tsp garlic powder

¼ tsp black pepper

¼ tsp paprika

1 tbsp olive oil

1 tbsp lemon juice

1 tbsp chopped fresh parsley

Lemon wedges for serving

Preparation

1. Preheat the oven to 400°F and line a baking sheet with parchment paper.

2. Combine the flour, garlic powder, black pepper, and paprika in a dish and dredge the tilapia fillets in the flour mixture.

3. Heat the olive oil in a large skillet on medium heat.

4. Add the tilapia fillets to the skillet and cook for 2 - 3 minutes on each side until lightly browned.

5. Transfer the tilapia fillets to the prepared baking sheet and drizzle the lemon juice over.
6. Bake in the oven for 10-12 minutes or until cooked through.
7. Garnish with chopped fresh parsley and serve with lemon wedges.

Nutritional value

Calories: 505 kcal | Carbohydrates: 9g |Protein: 67|Total Fat: 20g |Sugar: 1g | Cholesterol: 213mg | Sodium: 231mg |Dietary Fiber: 1g | Saturated Fat: 4g |

DASH Diet Beef Dishes

Below are healthy and delicious beef recipes for your DASH diet eating plan.

Beef Tacos

Preparation Time: 10 min
Cooking Time: 10 min | Servings: 4

Ingredients

2 tbsps extra virgin olive oil

½ cup chopped white onion, divided

1 cup chopped red bell pepper

1 large clove of garlic, minced

8 (6-inch) corn tortillas

4 radishes, thinly sliced

½ pound 95%-lean ground beef

½ tsp dried oregano

¼ tsp cracked black pepper

¾ cup chopped Roma tomato

1 tsp chopped jalapeño chile pepper (seeded for less heat)

4 tbsps chopped fresh cilantro

Juice of 1/2 lime

Preparation

1. Heat the olive oil in a large pan on medium heat. Add ¼ cup of onion, bell pepper, and garlic, and cook for 30 seconds. Then add the ground beef, breaking up large chunks with a spatula. Cook for 5 - 6 minutes until the meat is no longer pink. Add the oregano and black pepper while the meat cooks.

2. In a separate bowl, combine the remaining 1/4 cup chopped onion, tomato, chile pepper, cilantro, and lime juice to make a salsa topping.

3. Mix to incorporate evenly, and set aside.

4. Warm the tortillas in a flat pan over medium heat. Place two tortillas on four individual plates, scoop the beef mixture onto the tortillas, top with salsa and sliced radishes, and serve.

Nutritional value

Calories: 294kcal | Carbohydrates: 31g |Protein: 16g |Total Fat: 13g |Sugar: 2mg | Sodium: 73mg |Dietary Fiber: 5g| Saturated Fat: 3mg| Cholesterol: 33mg | Potassium: 318mg |

Beef Brisket

Preparation Time: 10 min
Cooking Time: 4 hrs | Servings: 6-8

Ingredients

4 pounds of beef brisket

1 can tomato-based sauce

1 cup beef broth

Freshly ground black pepper

1 tbsp extra virgin olive oil

1 medium onion

1 tsp dried thyme

4 garlic cloves, minced

Preparation

1. Prep your beef brisket by seasoning it with salt and pepper. Ensure it is evenly seasoned. All the while, preheat your oven to 425°F.

2. Heat a large roasting pan on medium heat with olive oil, place the seasoned brisket, and cook until it starts to brown on all sides.

3. Once it starts to brown, add onions, garlic, and thyme and cook for 1 minute before stirring in the tomatoes, vinegar, and stock. Cover the dish with foil and transfer it to the

oven. Cook for 3 hours until beef is cooked through. Allow resting for some minutes before slicing to eat.

Nutritional value

Calories: 229kcal | Carbohydrates: 33g |Protein: 37g |Total Fat: 31g |Sugar: 28mg | Sodium: 142mg |Dietary Fiber: 1g| Saturated Fat: 3mg|Cholesterol: 171mg |

Mexican Inspired Vegetable and Beef Skillet Meal

Preparation Time: 10 min

Cooking Time: 30 min | Servings: 8

Ingredients

½ pound lean ground beef

¾ cup onion, chopped

½ cup bell pepper

½ tablespoon chili powder

1 tbsp oregano

1 tsp salt

½ cup shredded cheese

1 cup rice, uncooked

1 cup tomatoes, chopped

1 cup mixed vegetables

2 cups water

Preparation

1. In a large skillet, brown beef on medium-high heat. Add onion and peppers and cook for 10 minutes until vegetables are tender.

2. Add rice, tomato, mixed vegetables, water, and spices. Mix and bring to a boil on medium heat for 20 minutes.

3. Add cheese and serve to enjoy.

Nutritional value

Calories: 315 kcal | Carbohydrates: 5g |Protein: 21g |Total Fat: 7g |Sugar: 3g | Sodium: 390mg

|Dietary Fiber: 1g| Saturated Fat: 9mg|Cholesterol: 81mg |

Beef Stroganoff

Preparation Time: 20 min

Cooking Time: 35 min | Servings: 6

Ingredients

½ cup onion, chopped

1 tbsp flour

½ tsp paprika

½ cup fat-free sour cream

½ pound boneless beef steak

4 cups hot cooked egg noodles

½ can fat-free cream of mushroom soup

½ cup of water

Preparation

1. Saute the onions over medium heat in a non-stick pan for 5 minutes. Add the beef and continue to cook for another 5 minutes until tender. Drain well and set aside.

2. In another pot, fill it with ¾ cup of water and boil. Add the noodles and cook until tender for 10 to 12 minutes. Drain the water once done.

3. Mix the soup, water, and flour in a saucepan over medium heat and stir for 5 minutes until it thickens. Add the soup mixture and paprika to the beef in the frying pan and cook over medium heat. Stir and once warmed through, remove from heat and add the sour cream.

4. Serve over noodles.

Nutritional value

Calories: 435 kcal | Carbohydrates: 37g |Protein: 20g |Total Fat: 23g | Sodium: 620mg |Dietary Fiber: 2g| Saturated Fat: 2mg|Cholesterol: 115mg

Sweet 'n Spicy Beef & Edamame Stir Fry

Preparation Time: 10 min
Cooking Time: 10 min | Servings: 4

Ingredients

8-ounce beef sirloin steak trimmed of fat and cut into skinny bite-size strips

4 tsp canola oil

2 tsp finely chopped fresh ginger

3 cups packaged fresh cut-up stir-fried vegetables

1 cup frozen shelled sweet soybeans

3 tbsp hoisin sauce

2 tbsp rice vinegar

1 tsp red chili paste

1 8.8-ounce pouch of cooked whole-grain brown rice

Preparation

1. Heat 2 tsp canola oil in a wok or skillet over medium-high heat. Stir in the ginger and cook for 15 to 20 seconds.

2. Add the vegetables and cook until tender-crisp for approx 4 - 5 minutes. Remove the vegetables from the pan and set aside.

3. Add the remaining 2 tsp of oil to the bowl and stir in the beef and edamame; cook until the beef is browned.

4. Return the vegetables to the wok. Mix the vinegar, chili paste, and hoisin in a bowl, and add to the beef mixture; toss well to coat.

5. Cook until heated through. Meanwhile, cook the rice according to the directions on the package.

6. Serve the beef with the rice to enjoy.

Nutritional value

Calories: 300kcal |Total Fat: 13g | Sodium: 570mg | Saturated Fat: 5mg|Cholesterol: 24mg| Sugar: 7g| Protein: 22g| Potassium: 505mg| Carbohydrate: 34g| Calcium: 101mg|

Peppered Sirloin Steak

Preparation Time: 15 min
Cooking Time: 20 min | Servings: 4

Ingredients

1 ½ lbs boneless beef sirloin steak, cut

2 tbsps catsup

½ tsp coarsely ground black pepper

1 ½ tsp snipped fresh rosemary or ½ tsp dried rosemary, crushed

1 ½ tsp snipped fresh basil or ½ tsp dried basil, crushed

⅛ tsp garlic powder

⅛ tsp ground cardamom (optional)

Grilled sweet peppers (optional)

Preparation

1. Mix the catsup, pepper, rosemary, garlic powder, basil, and cardamom (optional) in a bowl.

2. Marinade the steak with the mixture and leave for a while.

3. Place the steak on a grill with medium coals and leave for 6-7 minutes. Turn the steak onto the other side and leave for another 8-12 minutes until cooked.

4. Cut into your desired slices and serve garnished with fresh rosemary and grilled sweet peppers (optional).

Nutritional value

Calories: 497 kcal | Carbohydrates: 43 g |Protein: 64 g |Total Fat: 7.3g | Cholesterol:

94mg | Sodium: 847 mg | Protein:35g | Sugar:7g | Dietary Fiber:3g | Saturated Fat:7g | Potassium: 806mg |

One Pan Spaghetti

Preparation Time: 10 min

Cooking Time: 30 min | Servings: 4

Ingredients

½ lb lean ground beef

1 medium onion, chopped

3 ½ cups water

1 can (15-ounce.) tomato sauce

2 tsp dried oregano

½ tsp each of sugar, garlic powder, rosemary

¼ tsp pepper

2 cups (12 ounces.) of broken spaghetti

1 cup (4 ounces.) shredded parmesan cheese

Preparation

1. Place the meat and onion in an electric skillet on a heat of about 300F and allow to brown.
2. Remove the fat and pour the water and tomato sauce over the ingredients.
3. Toss in the spices and allow the mixture to boil.
4. Mix the spaghetti, cover with a lid, and simmer for 12-15 minutes.
5. Continue to stir regularly to prevent the ingredients from sticking to the bottom of the pan.
6. Once the spaghetti is cooked, sprinkle it with cheese and serve warm to enjoy.

Nutritional value

Calories: 295 kcal | Carbohydrates: 37g |Protein: 18g |Total Fat: 7g |Sugar: 4mg | Sodium: 319 mg |Dietary Fiber: 3g| Saturated Fat: 3mg|Cholesterol: 35mg |

Fireside Beef Stew

Preparation Time: 1 hr

Cooking Time: 3 hrs 45 min| Servings: 6

Ingredients

1-½ pounds boneless beef chuck pot roast

1 pound butternut squash, peeled

2 small onions, cut into wedges

2 cloves garlic, minced

1 can of low-sodium beef broth

1 can tomato sauce

2 tbsps Worcestershire sauce

1 tsp dry mustard

¼ tsp ground black pepper

⅛ tsp ground allspice

2 tbsps cold water

4 tsp cornstarch

1 9-ounce package of frozen Italian green beans

Preparation

1. Trim fat from meat. Cut meat into 1-inch pieces. Place meat in a slow cooker. Add squash, onions, and garlic. Stir in beef broth, tomato sauce, Worcestershire sauce, dry mustard, pepper, and allspice.
2. Cover and cook in a high-heat setting for 4 to 5 hours.
3. In a small bowl, combine cold water and cornstarch. Stir the cornstarch mixture and green beans in a slow cooker. Cover and cook for about 15 minutes more or until thickened.

Nutritional value

Calories: 208kcal | Carbohydrates: 17g |Protein: 28g |Total Fat: 5g |Potassium: 871mg | Sodium: 457mg |Calcium: 83g| Saturated Fat: 2mg|Cholesterol: 74mg |

Sirloin & Veggie Soup

Preparation Time: 10 min

Cooking Time: 40 min | Servings: 6

Ingredients

1 pound lean ground sirloin

1 tbsp. Oil

1 package of beef broth

1 bag frozen soup vegetables

2 tbsps Worcestershire sauce

1 small onion, diced

⅓ cup all-purpose flour

Preparation

1. Heat the oil in a large saucepan on medium heat. Add the onion and cook until tender. Next, add the ground beef to the pan and cook while breaking the beef into chunks with a spoon.

2. Add the flour and ⅔ cup of water, cover in a jar, shake until mixed evenly, then pour the flour mixture into the saucepan.

3. Add the beef broth and boil for 25 minutes.

4. Add vegetables to the pan and cook for 10 to 12 minutes. Add the Worcestershire sauce and stir it in.

Nutritional value

Calories: 373kcal | Carbohydrates: 20g |Protein: 28g |Total Fat: 18g |Sugar: 4mg |Dietary Fiber: 6g| Saturated Fat: 6g| Cholesterol: 78mg| Sodium: 1348mg|

Beef Salad Asian Style

Preparation Time: 10 min

Cooking Time: 20 min | Servings: 6

Ingredients

12-pound boneless beef sirloin steak

1 fresh jalapeno pepper, chopped

½ tsp finely shredded lime peel

1 tsp sugar

2 cloves garlic, minced

6 cups torn napa cabbage

½ cup red sweet pepper strips

¼ cup green onions, sliced

3 tbsps lime juice

2 tbsps low-sodium soy sauce

1 tbsp fresh cilantro

2 tsp toasted sesame oil

Preparation

1. Trim the steak and remove the excess fat. Place the steak on the rack of a broiler pan. Broil the steak for 13 to 15 minutes for medium doneness.

2. Leave for 5 minutes, then cut the steak into bite-size strips.

3. In the meantime, stir together the lime peel, lime juice, jalapeno pepper, soy sauce, sesame oil, cilantro, garlic, and sugar in a medium size mixing bowl.

4. Stir in the beef, and marinate in the refrigerator for 3 to 7 hours.

5. When ready to serve, toss the napa cabbage, green onions, and sweet pepper in a salad bowl.

6. Stir in the beef mix and arrange it in the center of the cabbage mix.

Nutritional value

Calories: 272kcal | Carbohydrates: 12.4g |Protein: 29.7g |Total Fat: 11.8g |Sugar: 6.7mg |Dietary Fiber: 6g| Saturated Fat: 3.1g| Cholesterol: 78mg| Sodium: 120mg|

Stuffed Bell Peppers

Preparation Time: 10 min

Cooking Time: 20 min | Servings: 4

Ingredients

½ pound lean ground beef

2 tbsps extra virgin olive oil

½ small white onion, chopped

1 cup chopped zucchini

1 tbsp chopped fresh parsley

2 small cloves garlic, minced

½ cup carrot, chopped

¼ tsp dried thyme

¼ tsp dried basil

1 can of kidney beans

4 large red bell peppers

2 cups low-sodium marinara sauce

Preparation

1. Preheat the oven to 350°F. Next, heat the olive oil in a pan on medium heat; add the onion, garlic, carrot, thyme, and basil. Cook for 1 to 2 minutes, then add the beef, breaking up clumps with a spatula.

2. Once the beef starts to brown, after about 5 to 6 minutes, add the zucchini, parsley, and kidney beans. Cook for 5 more minutes.

3. Cut the tops and remove the seeds and ribs to prepare the peppers. Fill each pepper with the meat mixture, and place in a baking dish so the peppers stand upright. Pour water into the dish to cover the bottom. Cover the pan with foil, and bake for 20 - 25 minutes.

4. Heat the marinara sauce in a small saucepan, and pour over each plated bell pepper before serving.

Nutritional value

Calories: 443 kcal | Carbohydrates: 46g |Protein: 20g |Total Fat: 22g |Sugar: 13mg |Dietary Fiber: 12g| Saturated Fat: 6g| Cholesterol: 43mg| Sodium: 988 mg|

Buttermilk Dressing on Steak Salad

Preparation Time: 10 min

Cooking Time: 20 min | Servings: 4

Ingredients

8-pound boneless beef top sirloin steak

8 cups mixed salad greens

2 medium carrots

1 medium yellow sweet pepper

1 cup cherry or pear-shaped tomatoes, halved

¼ cup finely shredded fresh basil

Preparation

1. Use a knife to trim the fat off the meat. Cut the meat into small strips. Use cooking spray or oil to coat a large skillet, and heat on medium heat.

2. Add the meat and cook for 3 minutes until the meat is tender.

3. Take off the skillet from the heat and stir in the basil.

4. Serve the meat mixture over the green mixture and drizzle with buttermilk dressing and tomato.

Nutritional value

Calories: 443 kcal | Carbohydrates: 17g |Protein: 19g |Total Fat: 10g |Sugar: 8mg |Dietary Fiber: 12g| Saturated Fat: 6g| Cholesterol: 32mg| Sodium: 387 mg|

Garlic Pork Chops

Preparation Time: 10 min

Cooking Time: 28 min | Servings: 2

Ingredients

4-pound lean boneless pork chops

4 cloves garlic, crushed

1 tsp paprika

Fresh black pepper

1 tbsp lime juice

1 tsp cumin

1 tsp chili powder

Preparation

1. Remove any fat from the pork. Season the pork with crushed garlic, spices, lime juice, and zest. Leave the pork for about 15-20 minutes to marinate well.

2. Place a foil on a broiler pan and lay the pork chops on the pan. Broil the pork chops for about 5 minutes per side until the chops brown. Serve to enjoy.

Nutritional value

Calories: 371 kcal | Carbohydrates: 1g |Protein: 14g |Total Fat: 35g |Sugar: 1mg |Dietary Fiber: 12g| Saturated Fat: 17g| Cholesterol: 100mg| Sodium: 478 mg|

French Style Roast Rack of Lamb

Preparation Time: 10 min

Cooking Time: 30 min | Servings: 4

Ingredients

2-pound French-style lamb rib roasts

1 cup dry red wine

2 cups soft wheat bread crumbs

2 cloves garlic, minced

1 tsp freshly grated nutmeg

3 tbsps olive oil

1 tbsp butter

1 tbsp snipped fresh rosemary

3 tbsps dried cranberries

½ tsp salt

½ tsp ground black pepper

Preparation

1. Preheat the oven to 450°F. Remove the lamb's membrane and excess fat. Place the lamb in a stable plastic bag on a baking tray. Mix the wine, nutmeg, and 1 clove of garlic into the bag just before sealing. Seal the bag and leave for over 4 hours up to 24 hours.

2. Heat 1 tbsp of oil and 1 tbsp butter in a skillet. Mix in the rosemary and garlic and cook for 1-2 minutes. Mix in the crumbs and leave for about 2-3 minutes.

3. Remove from the heat and mix in cranberries, seasonings, and oil. Remove the marinade from the lamb and leave the marinade aside. Place the lamb with the bone side facing down in a lined pan.

4. Spread the crumbs on top of the lamb and pour the kept-aside marinade onto the lamb. Roast for about 25-30 minutes until the meat is cooked.

5. Allow standing for 20 minutes before serving.

Nutritional value

Calories: 335 kcal | Carbohydrates: 0.5g |Protein: 46.7g |Total Fat: 16g |Sugar: 0.5mg | Saturated Fat: 7g| Cholesterol: 140mg| Sodium: 352.5mg|

Mighty Lean Cheese Burgers

Preparation Time: 10 min

Cooking Time: 20 min | Servings: 4

Ingredients

1 pound ground beef

½ tsp steak seasoning blend

4 seeded or whole wheat hamburger buns

2 tbsps. quick-cooking oats

4 slices of low-fat cheese

Lettuce leaves

Tomato slices (optional)

Preparation

1. Place the quick-cooking oats in a sealable bag and remove the excess air.

2. Seal the bag with the oats and use a rolling pin to smash the oats into one consistency.

3. Mix beef, oats, and steak seasoning well in a bowl. Form about ½ inch patties and keep the patties on a grid.

4. Leave to grill for about 12-13 minutes. Turn the patties on both sides to brown nicely. Place tomato and lettuce at the bottom and top up with a cheese slice and burger.

5. Tighten the sandwiches and serve.

Nutritional value

Calories: 146 kcal | Carbohydrates: 15g |Protein: 5g |Total Fat: 7g |Sugar: 1mg |Dietary Fiber: 2g| Saturated Fat: 2g| Cholesterol: 34mg| Sodium: 317mg|

Smoke Chops Caribbean Style

Preparation Time: 20 min

Cooking Time: 1 hr 20 min | Servings: 4

Ingredients

4 pork loin chops

6 to 8 pecan or cherry wood chunks

3 tsp Jamaican jerk seasoning

1 medium mango, peeled

¼ cup sliced green onion

1/2 tsp finely shredded orange peel

2 tsp orange juice

2 tbsp snipped fresh cilantro or parsley

Preparation

1. Soak chunks of wood in water for at least an hour before smoke-cooking; drain before cooking. Trim the fat off the chops with a knife.

2. Sprinkle jerk seasoning over the chops evenly, and rub in with your fingers.

3. Arrange the coals, water pan, and drained wood chunks in a smoker. Pour water into the pan, and place the pork chops on the grill directly over the water pan.

4. Cover and smoke for 1 hour 45 minutes s until the juices run clear.

5. Add the green onions, cilantro, mango, orange juice, orange peel, and a quarter of the jerk seasoning in a medium bowl to prepare the sauce. Then, stir together for 20 - 25 minutes.

6. Serve the mango and orange sauce over the pork chops.

7. Garnish the pork chops with cilantro sprigs if desired.

Nutritional value

Calories: 270 kcal |Protein: 29g |Total Fat: 16g |Sugar: 13mg |Dietary Fiber: 12g| Saturated Fat: 4g| Cholesterol: 90mg| Sodium: 64mg|

Quick Bean Chilli

Preparation Time: 10 min

Cooking Time: 20 min | Servings: 4

Ingredients

½ pound lean ground meat

1 can of kidney beans, drained

½ medium onion, chopped

1 can diced tomatoes with liquid

1 ½ tbsps. Chili powder

Preparation

1. Roast the ground meat and onions over medium-high heat in a large skillet.

2. Drain the fat, and add the tomatoes, chili powder, and beans to the skillet.

3. Reduce the heat, and cook for 10 - 12 minutes. Serve warm.

    Nutritional value

    Calories: 489 kcal | Carbohydrates: 27g |Protein: 26g |Total Fat: 22g |Sugar: 6mg |Dietary Fiber: 8g| Saturated Fat: 12g| Cholesterol: 43mg| Sodium: 988 mg|

Beef Shepard's Pie

Preparation Time: 20 min

Cooking Time: 20 min | Servings: 4

Ingredients

1 pound lean ground beef

1 medium onion, chopped

¾ cup low-sodium beef broth

2 large baking potatoes, diced

1/2 cup of low-fat milk

1 clove garlic, minced

2 tbsps flour

4 cups frozen mixed vegetables

½ cup shredded cheddar cheese

Preparation

1. In a saucepan, add the potatoes, cover with water, and boil for 15 min. Drain the potatoes, rinse, and mash. Add the milk;

2. Preheat oven to 375°F. Add garlic, onion, and meat in a large skillet, and cook until brown. Add the flour and constantly stir for 1 minute. Add the beef broth and vegetables to the skillet and cook until bubbly.

3. Add the mix to a baking dish. Spread the mashed potato and milk mixture over the vegetable and meat mixture. Sprinkle cheese on top and serve warm.

    Nutritional value

    Calories: 562 kcal | Carbohydrates: 32g |Protein: 21g |Total Fat: 40g |Sugar: 6mg |Dietary Fiber: 4g| Saturated Fat: 19g| Cholesterol: 107mg| Sodium: 855mg

DASH Diet Poultry Dishes

Turkey Meatloaf

Preparation Time: 15 min

Cooking Time: 1 hr 20 min | Servings: 6

Ingredients

1 ¼ pounds lean ground turkey

1 slice of 100% whole wheat bread, torn into small pieces

¼ cup low-sodium chicken broth

1 tsp Dijon mustard

1 tsp Worcestershire sauce

1 large egg

¼ cup onion, chopped

¼ cup bell pepper, chopped

¼ cup fresh parsley, chopped

1 tsp horseradish

½ tsp sea salt

¼ tsp black pepper

Preparation

1. Preheat the oven to 350°F. Put all the ingredients in a large bowl, and mix with your hands until the ingredients are evenly coated.

2. Lightly grease a deep baking dish with olive oil spray. Mold the meat mixture into a loaf, then place it in the pan. Bake uncovered for about an hour.

3. When the meatloaf is cooked, remove it from the oven and cool it for 10 minutes.

4. Slice and enjoy.

Nutritional value

Calories: 152 kcal | Carbohydrates: 15g |Protein: 19.6g |Total Fat: 7g |Sugar: 0.8mg |Sodium: 319mg |Dietary Fiber: 0.6g| Saturated Fat: 0.6mg|Cholesterol: 91mg|

Turkey Meatballs in Marinara Sauce

Preparation Time: 20 min

Cooking Time: 25 min | Servings: 4

Ingredients

1 pound lean ground turkey

½ small red onion

2 large cloves of garlic

¼ cup red bell pepper

3 tbsps fresh parsley, chopped

½ tsp chile pepper flakes

¼ cup whole wheat bread crumbs

⅛ tsp ground cumin

½ tsp dried Italian herbs

⅛ tsp cracked black pepper

1 egg

⅛ tsp sea salt

4 tbsps extra virgin olive oil

1 jar low-sodium marinara sauce

½ cup low-fat feta cheese

Preparation

1. Preheat the oven to 375°F. Combine all ingredients except the oil, marinara, and feta in a large bowl. Mix well until ingredients are incorporated into the meat. Roll the meat mixture into meatballs the size of golf balls.

2. Heat a large non-stick skillet on medium-high heat. Once hot, add the oil and then the meatballs in batches. Coat on each side, and place in an oven dish.

3. Once all the meatballs have been coated and placed in the dish, top with the marinara sauce and cover with foil. Bake for 20 to 25 minutes.

4. Once done, remove the foil from the dish, top the meatballs with the feta, and bake for another 4 minutes. Serve immediately to enjoy.

Nutritional value

Calories: 546 kcal | Carbohydrates: 32g |Protein: 32g |Total Fat: 33g |Sugar: 2mg | Sodium: 779 mg |Dietary Fiber: 6g| Saturated Fat: 8mg|Cholesterol: 143mg| Potassium: 852mg |

Chicken Pesto with Yellow Summer Squash

Preparation Time: 15 min

Cooking Time: 30 min | Servings: 4

Ingredients

4 medium skinless, boneless chicken breast

1 tbsp. olive oil

2 cups finely chopped zucchini or yellow summer squash

2 tbsps finely shredded Asiago or Parmesan cheese

2 tbsps homemade or purchased pesto

Preparation

1. Use a large non-stick skillet for cooking chicken in hot oil over medium heat for 5 minutes. Turn the chicken over and add the zucchini or squash to the skillet.

2. Cook for 5 minutes more until the chicken is no longer pink and the squash is tender-crisp; stir squash gently twice or thrice while cooking.

3. Plate the chicken and squash on 4 dishes and spread the pesto over the chicken. Sprinkle Parmesan or Asiago cheese on top.

Nutritional value

Calories: 144 kcal | Carbohydrates: 3g |Protein: 14g |Total Fat: 26g |Sugar: 2mg | Sodium: 181mg |Dietary Fiber: 1g| Saturated Fat: 2mg|Cholesterol: 39mg|

Turkey Dumpling & Vegetable Soup

Preparation Time: 15 min

Cooking Time: 45 min | Servings: 6

Ingredients

1 meaty leftover turkey

1 medium carrot

1 medium onion, chopped

6 cups low-sodium chicken broth

6 cups water

2 celery ribs, chopped

1 cup fresh or frozen green beans

1 package of frozen corn

1 package of frozen peas

2 cups biscuit or baking mix

⅔ cup low-fat milk

Preparation

1. Combine the soup stock ingredients in a Dutch oven and boil on low heat for 3 hours. Remove the turkey carcass and allow it to cool; then remove the meat from the bone.

2. Strain the broth and return to the oven. Add the carrots, beans, celery, and onions, and boil. Then, reduce heat, cover, and simmer until vegetables are soft. Add the reserved turkey, peas, and corn, and cook; reduce heat.

3. Mix the biscuit mixture and milk, and drop tsp at a time into the broth. Cover and let simmer until ready.

Nutritional value

Calories: 303 kcal | Carbohydrates: 29g |Protein: 14g |Total Fat: 13g |Sugar: 5mg | Sodium: 1161mg |Dietary Fiber: 3g| Saturated Fat: 2mg|Cholesterol: 76mg|

Quick Broccoli and Chicken Stir Fry

Preparation Time: 15 min

Cooking Time: 20 min | Servings: 3

Ingredients

1 pound boneless chicken breast

2 cups of cooked brown rice

⅓ cup orange juice

1 tbsp canola oil

2 cups of frozen broccoli florets

1 pound package of frozen snow peas

1 tbsp low-sodium soy sauce

1 tbsp Schezuan sauce

2 tsp cornstarch

2 cups shredded cabbage

1 tbsp sesame seeds (optional)

Preparation

1. Mix the Schezuan sauce, cornstarch, soy sauce, and orange juice; set aside. In a wok, heat the canola oil. Add the chicken to the wok and stir fry for 6 minutes until the meat has cooked through.

2. Add the broccoli, cabbage, snow peas, and sauce mix to the wok. Cook for 5 minutes until the vegetables are done.

3. Garnish with sesame seeds and serve with rice.

Nutritional value

Calories: 356 kcal | Carbohydrates: 41g |Protein: 33g |Total Fat: 26g |Sugar: 24mg |

Sodium: 3307mg |Dietary Fiber: 4g| Saturated Fat: 2mg|Cholesterol: 39mg|

Veggie Turkey Bake

Preparation Time: 25 min

Cooking Time: 45 min | Servings: 6

Ingredients

2 cups cooked brown or white rice

2 cups chopped cooked low-sodium turkey or chicken

½ cup finely shredded Parmesan cheese

2 cups sliced fresh mushrooms

¾ cup chopped red or yellow sweet pepper

½ cup onion, chopped

¼ cup all-purpose flour

¾ tsp salt

2 cloves garlic, minced

2 tbsps low-fat butter or margarine

½ tsp dried thyme, crushed

¼ tsp black pepper

2 cups fat-free milk

1 pound chopped spinach

Preparation

1. Stir the mushroom, sweet pepper, garlic, hot butter, and onion in a large skillet on medium heat until cooked.

2. Add the salt, thyme, flour, and black pepper to the skillet and stir it in. Stir in the milk slowly. Cook until it becomes bubbly and thick. Add the rice, turkey, spinach, and a quarter of the parmesan cheese, and stir it in.

3. Serve on a baking dish and sprinkle the balance of parmesan cheese; cover and bake in the oven at 350°F for 20 - 25 minutes.

4. Uncover the dish, and bake for 12 minutes until heated through. Take off from the oven and cool for 10 - 15 minutes. Serve warm.

Nutritional value

Calories: 287 kcal | Carbohydrates: 28g |Protein: 14g |Total Fat: 8g |Sugar: 6mg | Sodium: 393mg |Dietary Fiber: 3g| Saturated Fat: 3mg|Cholesterol: 53 mg|

Sweet Potato and Turkey Chowder

Preparation Time: 25 min
Cooking Time: 40 min | Servings: 8

Ingredients

1 can of low-sodium chicken broth

2 small ears of frozen corn-on-the-cob

1 large potato, peeled and chopped

12-pound cooked low-sodium turkey breast cubes

1 ½ cups fat-free milk

1 large sweet potato

⅛ tsp ground black pepper

¼ cup parsley

Preparation

1. Add the broth and potato to a saucepan and bring to a boil. Reduce heat to a lower setting and simmer, uncovered, until the potato is tender. Remove the pan from the heat.

2. Mash the potato until it is nearly smooth. Cut the kernels of the corn and set aside. Add the turkey milk, corn kernels, sweet potato, and pepper into the saucepan with the potato mixture; bring to a boil.

3. Reduce to a lower heat setting, cover, and cook until the sweet potato is soft.

4. Serve in bowls and sprinkle with parsley if desired.

Nutritional value

Calories: 362 kcal | Carbohydrates: 35g |Protein: 26g |Total Fat: 14g |Sugar: 13mg | Sodium: 2450mg |Dietary Fiber: 4g| Saturated Fat: 6mg|Cholesterol: 93mg|

Tomato Stuffed With Wild Rice and Chicken

Preparation Time: 10 min
Cooking Time: 30 min | Servings: 6

Ingredients

1 chicken breast

1 cup uncooked wild rice

1 cup low-sodium vegetable broth

1 cup water

4 large red tomatoes

2 cloves garlic, minced

½ cup shredded parmesan cheese

2 cloves garlic, minced

½ cup shredded parmesan cheese

2 tbsps fresh basil

2 tbsps olive oil

Preparation

1. Cook the wild rice according to the direction on the package, adding a cup of low-sodium vegetable broth and a cup of water.

2. Preheat the oven to 350°F. Grill the chicken until heated through. Slice the chicken into small pieces.

3. Cut the top off each tomato and scoop out the insides of the tomatoes.

4. Mix the chicken, garlic, basil, and parmesan cheese once the rice is cooked.

5. Use the rice filling to stuff the tomatoes. Sprinkle to tomatoes with the reserved parmesan cheese. Brush the tomatoes with olive oil and bake in the oven for 22 to 25 minutes.

Nutritional value

Calories: 162 kcal | Carbohydrates: 26g|Protein: 8g |Total Fat: 3g |Sugar: 3mg | Sodium: 206mg |Dietary Fiber: 3g| Saturated Fat: 2mg|Cholesterol: 7mg|

Cabbage and Chicken Stir Fry

Preparation Time: 20 min

Cooking Time: 25 min | Servings: 4

Ingredients

3 chicken breast

1 tbsp cornstarch

½ tsp ground ginger

¼ tsp garlic powder

1 tsp vegetable oil

3 cups green cabbage, shredded

½ cup water

1 tbsp low-sodium soy sauce

Preparation

1. Heat the vegetable oil in a pan. Cut the chicken breast into strips, add to the pan, and stir fry until heated through.

2. Next, add the cabbage to the pan and stir fry until the cabbage is tender-crisp. Mix the seasonings, cornstarch, water, and soy sauce in a small bowl until smooth.

3. Stir the mixture into the chicken mix. Cool for 2 minutes until the chicken is coated in the sauce.

Nutritional value

Calories: 418 kcal | Carbohydrates: 17g|Protein: 53g |Total Fat: 3g |Sugar: 6mg | Sodium: 835mg |Dietary Fiber: 6g| Saturated Fat: 2mg|Cholesterol: 146 mg|

Grilled Chicken with Black Bean Salsa

Preparation Time: 1 hr 15 min

Cooking Time: 10 min | Servings: 4

Ingredients

4 boneless, skinless chicken breasts

2 cups rinsed and drained canned black beans

1 large Granny Smith apple, chopped

1/2 small red onion, finely chopped

1 serrano chile pepper, seeded and thinly chopped

2 tbsps chopped fresh cilantro

Juice of 1 large lime

Juice of 1/2 orange

⅛ tsp sea salt

⅛ tsp cracked black pepper

Preparation

1. To make the salsa, combine all the ingredients (except the salt, pepper, and chicken) in a large bowl. Refrigerate for 1 hr to let the flavors meld.

2. Then, heat a grill or grill pan to medium-high heat. Add salt and pepper to chicken breasts. Put them on the grill, and cook for 4 to 6 minutes on each side or until the center of each is no longer pink.

3. Divide the salsa on top of the breasts, and serve.

Nutritional value

Calories: 251 kcal | Carbohydrates: 30g |Protein: 31g |Total Fat: 1g |Sugar: 5mg |

Sodium: 232 mg |Dietary Fiber: 9g| Saturated Fat: 0.2mg|Cholesterol: 55mg| Magnesium: 17% | Potassium: 431mg|

Orange Chicken and Brown Rice

Preparation Time: 10 min

Cooking Time: 15 min | Servings: 2

Ingredients

2 (4-ounce) boneless, skinless chicken breasts

1 tbsp sesame oil

1 tbsp extra virgin olive oil

½ cup coarsely chopped shiitake mushroom

¼ cup chopped white onion

1 large clove of garlic, minced

¼ tsp cracked black pepper

½ tsp grated orange zest

¼ tsp grated lemon zest

Juice of 1/2 orange

4 cups spinach

¼ tsp ground ginger

1 cup cooked brown rice

Preparation

1. Trim the fat from the chicken breasts and cut the chicken into small cubes. Then, heat sesame and olive oil in a medium pan over medium to high heat. Add the mushroom, onion, and garlic, and cook for 1 minute.

2. Add the chicken and season with pepper, ground ginger, orange, and lemon zest. Cook until the chicken has browned, about 4 to 5 minutes, and then add the orange juice.

3. Stir the chicken and scrape the bottom of the pan to incorporate flavors. Add the spinach, remove the pan from the heat, and immediately cover it to steam it.

4. Divide the cooked brown rice between two dishes and top with orange chicken.

Nutritional value

Calories: 334 kcal | Carbohydrates: 25g |Protein: 27g |Total Fat: 15g |Sugar: 5mg | Sodium: 282mg |Dietary Fiber: 4g| Saturated Fat: 2mg|Cholesterol: 55mg| Magnesium: 20% | Potassium: 498mg|

Vegetables and Turkey Stir Fry

Preparation Time: 10 min

Cooking Time: 20 min | Servings: 2

Ingredients

3 cups cooked brown rice

1 tbsp oil

½ tsp salt

Thin slices of ginger root, minced

1 clove garlic, peeled and chopped, or 1/8 teaspoon garlic powder

1 cup turkey, cut into ½-inch cubes

2 cups chopped vegetables, fresh, frozen, or canned, such as celery, mushrooms, water chestnuts, bok choy

½ tsp sugar

Preparation

1. First, heat oil in a large skillet over medium heat. Add salt, ginger root, garlic, turkey, and vegetables. Stir-fry for 1 minute. Reduce heat to prevent scorching. Add sugar.

2. When vegetables are tender, remove the pan from heat. If vegetables are firm, add 1-2 tsp of water and cook for 2 more minutes or until tender. Serve over rice or noodles.

Nutritional value

Calories: 290 kcal | Carbohydrates: 21g |Protein: 37g |Total Fat: 6g |Sugar: 5mg |

Sodium: 1079 mg |Dietary Fiber: 6g| Saturated Fat: 1mg|Cholesterol: 85mg| Potassium: 549 mg|

Turkey Fajitas Bowl

Preparation Time: 10 min

Cooking Time: 10 min | Servings: 2

Ingredients

½ pound turkey breast

½ cup shredded cheddar cheese for topping

4- 8 inches corn tortillas

2 tbsps olive oil

1 tsp lemon juice

1 clove Garlic, crushed

¾ tsp fresh chile pepper, or dried to taste

½ tsp dried oregano leaves

½ large yellow bell pepper

½ large green pepper cut into 1-inch pieces

1 medium tomato, cut into 12 wedges

4 tbsps salsa for topping

Preparation

1. Cut turkey into thin slices and then into strips about 3/4 inch wide. In a medium bowl, combine 1 tbsp of the oil with the lemon juice, garlic, fresh Chile pepper, and oregano. Add turkey and stir to coat. Let marinate for ½ hour.

2. Then, heat the remaining 1 tbsp oil in a non-stick skillet over medium-high heat. Add yellow and green peppers, and stir fry for 2 minutes. Add turkey strips and stir fry for another 3 minutes. Stir in tomato and heat.

3. Warm tortillas in a skillet and use them as a base. Fill the tortilla or tostada bowl and top with cheese and salsa.

Nutritional value

Calories: 350 kcal | Carbohydrates: 32g |Protein: 44g |Total Fat: 62g |Sugar: 4mg | Sodium: 280mg |Dietary Fiber: 4g| Saturated Fat: 1.5mg|Cholesterol: 100mg|

Italian Herbed Turkey Cutlets

Preparation Time: 5 min

Cooking Time: 30 min | Servings: 4

Ingredients

3 small cloves garlic, minced

2 tbsps chopped fresh rosemary

2 tbsps chopped fresh parsley

1 ½ tsp chopped fresh sage

½ tsp cracked black pepper

4 (4-ounce) boneless, skinless turkey cutlets

Grated zest of 1 large lemon

1 cup low-sodium vegetable broth

Preparation

1. Preheat the oven to 375°F. Mix the garlic, rosemary, parsley, sage, and pepper in a small bowl. Rub a generous amount of the herb mixture on both sides of each cutlet.

2. Place the turkey cutlets in a 9-by-13-inch baking dish, top with lemon zest, and add the vegetable broth. Next, cover with foil, and bake for 20 to 25 minutes.

3. Take out the foil during the last 5 minutes of baking to brown the tops of the cutlets. Remove from the oven and serve.

Nutritional value

Calories: 129 kcal | Carbohydrates: 7g |Protein: 19.6g |Total Fat: 2g |Sugar: 5mg | Sodium: 1188 mg |Dietary Fiber: 1g| Saturated Fat: 0.6mg|Cholesterol: 49mg| Magnesium: 6% | Potassium: 373mg|

Peppers Stuffed with Turkey & Vegetables

Preparation Time: 20 min

Cooking Time: 40 min | Servings: 2

Ingredients

10-ounce ground turkey

1 cup cooked brown rice

3 bell peppers (green, red, or yellow)

1 tsp Italian seasoning (or basil and oregano leaves)

½ tsp garlic powder

¼ tsp each salt and pepper

½ onion

1 cup sliced mushrooms

1 chopped zucchini (about 1 cup)

1 can (14.5 ounces) diced tomatoes with liquid

Preparation

1. Cook the rice or prepare instant rice according to package directions. Preheat the oven to 350°F.

2. Cook the turkey in the large skillet over medium heat until no longer pink. Add seasonings during the last few minutes. Add onion, mushrooms, and zucchini to the skillet. Saute until tender. Mix in tomatoes and rice. Remove from heat.

3. Cut the peppers in half. Remove the stem and seeds. Put pepper halves in a baking dish and fill with the skillet mixture. Cover the baking dish with foil. Bake at 350 degrees for 40 to 50 minutes or until peppers are tender when poked with a fork.

Nutritional value

Calories: 279 kcal | Carbohydrates: 10g |Protein: 25g |Total Fat: 16g |Sugar: 6mg | Sodium: 472mg |Dietary Fiber: 3g| Saturated Fat: 3mg| Cholesterol: 84mg| Potassium: 657 mg|

Pear Chicken Curry

Preparation Time: 15 min

Cooking Time: 20 min | Servings: 2

Ingredients

3 chicken breasts (1 ½ pounds), halved, boneless, skinless, cut into 1-inch cubes

2 ripe pears divided

1 tbsp vegetable oil

1 cup diced onion

1 tbsp curry powder

1 tsp minced garlic

1 teaspoon salt

¾ tsp ground ginger

¾ tsp ground cinnamon

¼ tsp ground black pepper

1 can (14 ounces) of light coconut milk

⅓ cup raisins (optional)

Preparation

1. Peel and core 1 pear; puree and set aside.

2. Heat the vegetable oil in a pan. Add onion, curry powder, garlic, salt, ginger, cinnamon, and pepper and sauté 5 minutes, stirring occasionally, until onions are transparent.

3. Add chicken, and continue to sauté for 5 minutes, occasionally stirring, until browned. Add pureed pear, coconut milk, and raisins. Simmer for 5 minutes.

4. Core and cut the remaining pear into ½-inch cubes and add to the curry. Simmer for 5 minutes and serve.

Nutritional value

Calories: 360 kcal | Carbohydrates: 21g |Protein: 26g |Dietary Fiber: 3g| Sodium: 417

mg | Saturated Fat: 1g | Cholesterol: 13mg | Sugar: 10g | Potassium: 241 mg | Total Fat: 4g

Mediterranean Lemon Chicken and Potatoes

Preparation Time: 15 min

Cooking Time: 45 min | Servings: 2

Ingredients

1 ½ pound chicken breasts, cut into cubes

1 pound of potatoes, cut into cubes

1 medium onion, coarsely chopped

½ cup reduced-fat Greek or olive oil vinaigrette

¼ cup lemon juice

1 tsp dry oregano

1 tsp minced garlic

½ cup chopped tomato

Preparation

1. Mix all ingredients except tomatoes in a large bowl. Place equal amounts onto 4 large squares of heavy-duty foil. Fold in the top and sides of each to enclose the filling, leaving room for air to circulate.

2. Grill over medium heat for about 25 - 30 minutes or until chicken is cooked and potatoes are soft.

3. Carefully open packets and sprinkle equal amounts of tomato over each.

Nutritional value

Calories: 974 kcal | Carbohydrates: 49g |Protein: 99g |Total Fat: 40g |Sugar: 6mg | Sodium: 797mg |Dietary Fiber: 7g| Saturated Fat: 8mg| Potassium: 2785mg|

Chicken and Cabbage Toss

Preparation Time: 10 min

Cooking Time: 10 min | Servings: 4

Ingredients

4 medium skinless, boneless chicken breast halves

1 tbsp cooking oil

4 cups shredded green cabbage

4 cups shredded red cabbage

4 cups shredded Napa cabbage

1 tbsp. thinly shredded lemon peel

1 tsp. salt

¾ tsp pepper

Preparation

1. Cut the chicken breast into thin, small strips. Heat the cooking oil over medium-high heat in a wok or large skillet. Add half of the chicken strip to the wok and stir-fry for 3 min until no pink remains. Then remove it from the wok.

2. Add the other half of the chicken strips to the wok and repeat.

3. Allow the cooked chicken to cool slightly, and then combine it with the cabbages, lemon peel, salt, and pepper in a bowl.

4. Toss it gently to mix well.

Nutritional value

Calories: 328 kcal | Carbohydrates: 15g |Protein: 25g |Total Fat: 15g |Sugar: 7mg | Sodium: 278 mg |Dietary Fiber: 6g| Saturated Fat: 6mg|Cholesterol: 115mg|

Grilled Chicken with Crunchy Apple Salsa

Preparation Time: 10 min

Cooking Time: 50 min | Servings: 4

Ingredients

Salsa:

2 cups chopped, cored Gala apples

1 Anaheim chili pepper, seeded and chopped

½ cup chopped onion

¼ cup lime juice

Salt and black pepper

Grilled Chicken:

2 whole boneless, skinless chicken breasts

¼ cup dry white wine

¼ cup apple juice

½ tsp grated lime zest

½ tsp salt

⅛ tsp black pepper

Preparation

1. Prepare Salsa: In a medium bowl, combine apples, chili pepper, onion, lime juice, and salt and pepper to taste; cover and set aside while preparing chicken.

2. Prepare Grilled Chicken: In a large bowl, combine white wine, apple juice, lime zest, salt, and pepper. Cut chicken breasts in half for a total of four pieces. Add chicken and turn to coat with mixture; cover and refrigerate for 30 to 40 minutes.

3. Heat the grill. Drain and discard the chicken marinade. Grill chicken until cooked through; serve with salsa.

Nutritional value

Calories: 763 kcal | Carbohydrates: 23.4g |Protein: 103g |Sodium: 360mg |Cholesterol: 312mg| Fat:4g | Saturated Fat: 1g | Sugar:8g | Dietary Fiber: 2mg|

DASH Diet Side Dishes

Try these delicious side dish recipes to help reduce high blood pressure and for a healthy lifestyle.

Brown Rice Pilaf

Preparation Time: 10 min

Cooking Time: 45 min | Servings: 8

Ingredients

1 ⅛ cups dark brown rice, rinsed and drained

2 cups water

¼ cup chopped pistachio nuts

¼ cup dried apricots, chopped

¾ tsp salt, divided

¼ tsp saffron threads or ground turmeric

½ tsp grated orange zest

3 tbsps fresh orange juice

1 ½ tbsps pistachio oil or canola oil

Preparation

1. Combine the rice, water, ¼ tsp of salt, and saffron in a saucepan over high heat. Bring to a boil. Then, decrease the heat to low, cover, and simmer until the rice is tender. Move to a large bowl and keep warm.

2. Combine the orange zest, juice, oil, and the remaining ½ tsp salt in a small bowl. Whisk to blend. Pour the orange mixture over the warm rice. Add the nuts and apricots and toss gently to mix and coat. Serve immediately to enjoy.

Nutritional value

Calories: 153 kcal | Carbohydrates: 24g |Protein: 3g |Total Fat: 5mg |Sugar: 0mg | Sodium: 222mg |Dietary Fiber: 2g| Saturated Fat: 3mg|Cholesterol: 0mg|

Easy Tzatziki Greek Yogurt Sauce

Preparation Time: 20 min

Cooking Time: 1 hr | Servings: 6

Ingredients

2 cups low-fat Greek yogurt

2 large cloves garlic, chopped

¼ cup English cucumber, diced

¼ cup fresh mint leaves, chopped

Juice of ½ lemon

1 tbsp extra virgin olive oil

¼ tsp cracked black pepper

⅛ tsp sea salt

Preparation

1. Mix all the chopped ingredients in a large bowl with the yogurt, lemon juice, and oil. Mix well, and add salt and pepper.

2. Leave the mixture for 30 minutes to an hour before serving so the flavors properly blend.

Nutritional value

Calories: 51 kcal | Carbohydrates: 4g |Protein: 3g |Total Fat: 0mg |Sugar: 4mg | Sodium: 57mg |Dietary Fiber: 0.1g| Saturated Fat: 0.8mg|Cholesterol: 3mg| Potassium: 139|

Shrimp Ceviche

Preparation Time: 30 min

Cooking Time: 2 hrs | Servings: 4

Ingredients

½ pound raw shrimp

2 lemons, zest, and juice

2 limes, zest, and juice

2 tsp olive oil

2 tsp cumin

¼ diced serrano chili pepper

1 peeled cucumber

¼ cup chopped cilantro

1/2 cup diced red onion

1 cup diced tomato

2 tsp minced garlic

1 cup black beans, cooked

Preparation

1. Put shrimp in a pan and cover with lemon and lime juice. Leave in the refrigerator for at least 4 hours or until the shrimp is firm and white.

2. Mix the remaining ingredients in a separate bowl and set aside while the shrimp is cold cooking. Mix shrimp and citrus juice with the remaining ingredients when ready to serve. Serve with baked tortilla chips.

Nutritional value

Calories: 98 kcal | Carbohydrates: 10g |Protein: 7g |Total Fat: 4mg |Sugar: 0mg | Sodium: 167mg |Dietary Fiber: 3g| Saturated Fat: 1mg|Cholesterol: 36mg|

Artichoke, Spinach, and White Bean Dip

Preparation Time: 15 min
Cooking Time: 35 min | Servings: 8

Ingredients

2 cups artichoke hearts

1 tbsp black pepper

2 tbsps grated parmesan cheese

½ cup low-fat sour cream

4 cups chopped spinach

1 tsp minced dried thyme

2 cloves garlic, minced

1 tbsp minced fresh parsley

1 cup cooked white beans

Preparation

1. Heat oven to 350°F.

2. Mix all ingredients. Put in a glass or ceramic dish and bake for 30 minutes.

3. Serve with vegetables or whole-grain bread or crackers.

Nutritional value

Calories: 123 kcal | Carbohydrates: 16g |Protein: 8g |Total Fat: 3mg |Sugar: 0mg | Sodium: 114mg |Dietary Fiber: 7.5g| Saturated Fat: 1.5mg|Cholesterol: 6mg|

Balsamic Roasted Vegetables

Preparation Time: 10 min
Cooking Time: 25 min | Servings: 4

Ingredients

2 cups chopped vegetables (such as carrots, sweet potatoes, broccoli, and red onion)

2 tablespoons balsamic vinegar

2 tablespoons olive oil

1 teaspoon dried thyme

Salt and black pepper to taste

Preparation

1. Preheat oven to 400°F.

2. Line a baking sheet with parchment paper.

3. In a large bowl, combine the chopped vegetables with balsamic vinegar, olive oil, and thyme. Add salt and black pepper to taste.

4. Spread the vegetables evenly on the baking sheet.

5. Roast in the oven for 25 minutes or until the vegetables are tender.

6. Take away from the oven, serve, and enjoy!

Nutritional value

Calories: 110 kcal | Carbohydrates: 18g | Protein: 3g |Total Fat: 4g |Sugar: 10g | Sodium: 53 mg | Dietary Fiber: 4g| Saturated Fat: 1mg| Cholesterol: 0mg

Corn Pudding

Preparation Time: 10 min

Cooking Time: 30 min | Servings: 8

Ingredients

3 cups water

3 cups skim milk

2 cups coarse cornmeal (or polenta)

¼ cup maple syrup

¼ tsp cinnamon

⅛ tsp clove

⅛ tsp ginger

⅛ tsp nutmeg

½ cup raisins

Preparation

1. In the saucepan, bring water and milk to a boil. Add cornmeal and stir to remove lumps. Bring back to a boil. Then turn the heat low and cover, occasionally stirring for 10 to 15 minutes.

2. Shut off the heat and stir in the remaining ingredients. Allow resting for 10 to 15 minutes. Stir and serve.

Nutritional value

Calories: 213kcal | Carbohydrates: 45g |Protein: 6g |Total Fat: 1mg |Sugar: 7mg | Sodium: 44mg |Dietary Fiber: 2g| Saturated Fat: 1mg|Cholesterol: 6mg|

Thyme Roasted Beets

Preparation Time: 20 min

Cooking Time: 40 min | Servings: 4

Ingredients

2 medium golden or red beets, washed and trimmed

1 tbsp olive oil

1 tsp fresh thyme

¼ tsp salt

¼ tsp ground black pepper

Preparation

1. Heat the oven to 400°F. Then, Wrap the beets in aluminum foil and bake for 40 minutes or until tender. Set aside to cool slightly.

2. Peel the beets and cut beets into medium-sized chunks. Combine the cooked beets, oil, thyme, salt, and pepper in a medium bowl.

3. Put on a baking sheet and roast in the oven for 5 to 10 minutes until hot.

Nutritional value

Calories: 59 kcal | Carbohydrates: 7g |Protein: 1g |Total Fat: 3mg |Sugar: 5mg | Sodium: 176mg |Dietary Fiber: 2g| Saturated Fat: 0mg|Cholesterol: 0mg|

Honey-Glazed Sweet Potatoes

Preparation Time: 15 min

Cooking Time: 1 hr | Servings: 4

Ingredients

2 pounds sweet potatoes

¼ cup water

2 tbsps honey

1 tbsp olive oil

2 tbsps brown sugar

Cracked black pepper

Preparation

1. Heat the oven to 375°F. Meanwhile, lightly coat a baking pan with cooking spray.

2. For the sauce: add water, brown sugar, olive oil, and honey in a bowl and whisk until smooth. Put a layer of sweet potatoes in the baking pan and coat the sauce over the potatoes.

3. Cover and bake for 45 minutes until tender. Once done, remove the cover and bake until the glaze is set for another 15 minutes.

4. Then, transfer to a serving plate and garnish with pepper.

Nutritional value

Calories: 150 kcal | Carbohydrates: 31g |Protein: 3g |Total Fat: 2mg |Sugar: 29mg | Sodium: 100mg |Dietary Fiber: 6g| Saturated Fat: 3mg|Cholesterol: 6mg|

Fresh Fruit Kebabs

Preparation Time: 15 min
Cooking Time: 15 min | Servings: 2

Ingredients

4 wooden skewers
6 ounces of low-fat lemon yogurt
1 tsp lime zest
4 pineapple chunks
1 tsp fresh lime juice
4 strawberries
1 unit kiwi
½ banana
4 grapes

Preparation

1. Whisk the yogurt, lime juice, and zest in a small bowl. You can cover and refrigerate until needed.

2. Thread 1 piece of fruit onto the skewer. Repeat the process until all the fruit is gone. To enjoy, serve with lemon-lime dip.

Nutritional value

Calories: 140 kcal | Carbohydrates: 33g |Protein: 3g |Total Fat: 2mg |Sugar: 22mg | Sodium: 30mg |Dietary Fiber: 4g| Saturated Fat: 1mg|Cholesterol: 5mg|

Tropical Salsa

Preparation Time: 20 min
Cooking Time: 40 min | Servings: 4

Ingredients

1 large mango, peeled, pitted, and diced
½ cup diced red onion
3 tablespoons chopped fresh cilantro
1/2 large jalapeño chile pepper, finely chopped
2 large avocados, peeled, pitted, and diced
1 small red bell pepper, diced
2 large Roma tomatoes, diced
Lime juice
⅛ tsp sea salt
⅛ tsp cracked black pepper

Preparation

1. Combine all the ingredients in a bowl.

2. Before serving, refrigerate for at least 20 minutes to blend the flavors.

Nutritional value

Calories: 82 kcal | Carbohydrates: 9g |Protein: 1g |Total Fat: 6mg |Sugar: 3mg | Sodium: 35mg |Dietary Fiber: 3g| Saturated Fat: 0.8mg|Cholesterol: 0mg|

Chipotle Dip

Preparation Time: 10 min
Cooking Time: 20 min | Servings: 4

Ingredients

1 tbsp extra virgin olive oil
½ small white onion, chopped

2 large cloves garlic, minced

2 teaspoons canned chipotle pepper sauce

1 cup low-fat plain Greek yogurt

⅛ tsp sea salt

⅛ tsp cracked black pepper

Preparation

1. Heat the oil in a small pan on medium-high heat. Once hot, add the onion and garlic, and cook for a few minutes until the onion is translucent. Add the chipotle sauce, and mix it with the onion and garlic. Remove the pan from the heat.

2. Transfer the mixture to another bowl, and add the yogurt. Mix and add salt and pepper to taste. Refrigerate for 20 to 30 minutes before serving.

Nutritional value

Calories: 78 kcal | Carbohydrates: 7g |Protein: 4g |Total Fat: 5mg |Sugar: 4mg | Sodium: 98mg |Dietary Fiber: 0.4g| Saturated Fat: 6mg|Cholesterol: 4mg|

French Onion Dip

Preparation Time: 10 min

Cooking Time: 10 min | Servings: 4

Ingredients

2 tbsp extra virgin olive oil

2 tbsps Worcestershire sauce

⅛ tsp sea salt

⅛ tsp cracked black pepper

1 small white onion, chopped

2 cloves garlic, minced

1 cup low-fat plain Greek yogurt

1 cup low-fat sour cream

Minced chives for garnish

Preparation

1. Heat the oil in a small pan on low heat. Then, add the onion and garlic, and saute until the onion becomes brown and tender.

2. In a separate bowl, combine the yogurt, sour cream, Worcestershire sauce, and salt and pepper to taste. Add the onion and garlic mixture, and mix well. Garnish with minced chives.

Nutritional value

Calories: 161 kcal | Carbohydrates: 9g |Protein: 5g |Total Fat: 12mg |Sugar: 6mg | Sodium: 140mg |Dietary Fiber: 0.1g| Saturated Fat: 6mg|Cholesterol: 28mg|

Spinach Artichoke Dip

Preparation Time: 10 min

Cooking Time: 10 min | Servings: 4

Ingredients

3 cups spinach

2 cans artichoke hearts, coarsely chopped

1 large clove garlic, f minced

1 cup low-fat plain Greek yogurt

½ cup low-fat sour cream

¼ tsp dried parsley

¼ tsp dried basil

½ cup shredded Parmesan cheese

½ cup shredded part-skim mozzarella cheese

⅛ tsp sea salt

⅛ tsp cracked black pepper

Preparation

1. Preheat the oven to 400°F. Fill a medium pot with water, and bring it to a boil. Add the spinach, and after 1 minute, drain the spinach in a colander. Let it cool, and then wring the water out by hand.

2. Transfer to a cutting board, and chop coarsely. Add the spinach, artichoke hearts, garlic, yogurt, sour cream, dried herbs, salt, and pepper in a food processor, and half of both kinds of cheese. Pulse the mixture a few times to the desired consistency. Process in batches if necessary.

3. Transfer the mixture to an ovenproof serving dish, and spread it evenly with a rubber spatula. Top with the rest of the Parmesan and mozzarella. Bake 15 - 20 minutes, or until the cheeses on top completely melt and start to brown. Remove from the oven, and serve immediately.

Nutritional value

Calories: 263 kcal | Carbohydrates: 18g |Protein: 20g |Total Fat: 14mg |Sugar: 4mg | Sodium: 537mg |Dietary Fiber: 6g| Saturated Fat: 8mg|Cholesterol: 42mg|

Roasted Zucchini Crostini Dip

Preparation Time: 10 min
Cooking Time: 15 min | Servings: 6

Ingredients

2 large green zucchini, sliced

¼ tsp cracked black pepper

¼ tsp chile pepper flakes

1 large yellow zucchini, sliced

¼ tsp dried basil

⅛ cup extra virgin olive oil

¼ cup grated Parmesan cheese

½ small red onion, coarsely chopped

2 large cloves garlic, whole

½ cup balsamic vinegar

1 tbsp water

Preparation

1. Preheat the oven to 400°F. Arrange the sliced zucchini and chopped onion in a roasting pan with the garlic. Drizzle with balsamic vinegar, and season with black pepper, chili pepper flakes, and basil. Roast for 10 - 12 minutes or until the onion is soft and starting to brown.

2. Transfer the cooked veggies to a blender or food processor. While blending, slowly drizzle in olive oil, alternating with Parmesan. Add up to 2 tablespoons of water while mixing for a thinner consistency.

Nutritional value

Calories: 98 kcal | Carbohydrates: 7g |Protein: 7g |Total Fat: 7mg |Sugar: 1mg | Sodium: 85mg |Dietary Fiber: 2g| Saturated Fat: 2mg|Cholesterol: 3mg|

Spicy Sun-Roasted Tomato Hummus

Preparation Time: 20 min
Cooking Time: 40 min | Servings: 8

Ingredients

2 cans garbanzo beans

½ tsp sea salt

½ tsp cracked black pepper

5 tbsps extra virgin olive oil

¼ cup tahini paste

2 tbsps lemon juice

2 large cloves of garlic

2 tbsps sun-roasted tomato slices

1 dried red chili

Preparation

1. Place the beans, tahini, lemon juice, garlic, tomato, chile, salt, and pepper in a food processor. While processing, drizzle in the oil

until there are no large pieces and the hummus is smooth.

2. Transfer to a serving dish, top with dried oregano and a drizzle of olive oil, and serve.

Nutritional value

Calories: 262 kcal | Carbohydrates: 7g |Protein: 7g |Total Fat: 14mg |Sugar: 1mg | Sodium: 471mg |Dietary Fiber: 6g| Saturated Fat: 2mg|Cholesterol: 3mg|

Grilled Rustic Corn

Preparation Time: 10 min

Cooking Time: 20 min | Servings: 4

Ingredients

4 large ears of corn

¼ tsp sea salt

¼ tsp cracked black pepper

4 tbsps extra virgin olive oil

4 large cloves garlic, minced finely

Preparation

1. Peel the husks and remove the silk from each ear of corn. Mix the salt and pepper in a bowl. Brush the kernels with oil, sprinkle each with minced garlic, and then the salt and pepper mixture.

2. Fold the husks back over the corn, then grill over low heat until cooked through, 12 to 15 minutes, turning occasionally.

Nutritional value

Calories: 249 kcal | Carbohydrates: 28g |Protein: 5g |Total Fat: 16mg |Sugar: 5mg | Sodium: 167mg |Dietary Fiber: 4g| Saturated Fat: 2mg|Cholesterol: 0mg|

Grilled Sweet Potato Steak Fries

Preparation Time: 20 min

Cooking Time: 40 min | Servings: 4

Ingredients

1 pound sweet potatoes, unpeeled

½ tsp cayenne pepper

¼ tsp cracked black pepper

4 tbsps extra virgin olive oil

½ tsp ground cumin

¼ tsp sea salt

Preparation

1. Fill a large pot with water, then bring it to a boil. Add the sweet potatoes, and boil for 10 to 12 minutes. Strain the potatoes, and let them cool. Once cooled, cut them in half lengthwise.

2. Brush oil onto each slice, and sprinkle with cumin, cayenne, and black pepper. Arrange on the grill, and cook for 1 to 2 minutes per side.

3. Remove from the heat, season with salt.

Nutritional value

Calories: 258 kcal | Carbohydrates: 32g |Protein: 7g |Total Fat: 14mg |Sugar: 0mg | Sodium: 166 mg |Dietary Fiber: 4g| Saturated Fat: 2mg|Cholesterol: 3mg|

Grilled Collard Greens

Preparation Time: 10 min

Cooking Time: 10 min | Servings: 6

Ingredients

1 pound collard greens

4 tbsp red wine vinegar

5 tbsps extra virgin olive oil

¼ tsp sea salt

¼ tsp cracked black pepper

Preparation

1. Cut off the thick ends of the stems, wash the greens, and pat them completely dry. Lay each leaf directly on a hot grill. After 30 seconds, flip each leaf over. Remove the leaves when they blacken, put them in a large pot, and cover them with a lid.

2. After all the leaves have been grilled, let them sit in the covered pot for about 5 minutes to continue streaming. Remove the leaves from the pot, and cut them into 2- inch-wide pieces.

3. Place them back in the pot, and top with the vinegar, oil, salt, and pepper to taste. Serve warm or chilled.

Nutritional value

Calories: 135 kcal | Carbohydrates: 7g |Protein: 1g |Total Fat: 14mg |Sugar: 0.2mg | Sodium: 156mg |Dietary Fiber: 2g| Saturated Fat: 2mg|Cholesterol: 0mg|

Kale and Butternut Squash Sauté

Preparation Time: 10 min

Cooking Time: 25 min | Servings: 6

Ingredients

1 pound kale

1 pound pre-cut butternut squash

½ cup toasted pine nuts

Pinch of chile pepper flakes

⅛ tsp sea salt

⅛ tsp cracked black pepper

4 tbsps grated cheese

2 tbsps extra virgin olive oil

1 tbsp shallot, finely chopped

2 large cloves garlic, minced

Preparation

1. Chop off and discard the rough ends of the kale. Wash, dry thoroughly, and coarsely chop the kale. Heat the olive oil in a large pan on medium heat. Add the squash, and cook for 15 to 20 minutes or until browned.

2. Add the kale, cook for 1 minute, and then add the shallot, garlic, chile flakes, salt, and pepper. Saute for 3 minutes, add the pine nuts and cook for 1 min.

3. Top with cheese and serve.

Nutritional value

Calories: 144 kcal | Carbohydrates: 21g |Protein: 5g |Total Fat: 7mg |Sugar: 1mg | Sodium: 85mg |Dietary Fiber: 6g| Saturated Fat: 2mg|Cholesterol: 3mg|

DASH Diet Beans & Grains

Easy Black Bean Soup

Preparation Time: 10 min

Cooking Time: 30 min | Servings: 2

Ingredients

2 tsp vegetable oil

1 medium onion, chopped

1-½ tsp cinnamon

2 cans (19 ounces each) of black beans with liquid

1 package (32 ounces) of low-sodium chicken broth

1 large sweet potato, diced

Plain Greek-style yogurt (optional)

Preparation

1. In a saucepan, heat oil over medium heat. Add onion and cinnamon, and cook for 6 minutes. Stir in beans, chicken broth, and sweet potato. Bring mixture to a boil; decrease heat and simmer for 10 minutes.

2. Let soup cool for 5 minutes, and puree in a blender in two batches until smooth. Reheat on low until warm before serving. Top with yogurt, if desired.

Nutritional value

Calories: 180 kcal | Carbohydrates: 27.4g |Protein: 11.5g |Total Fat: 3.7g |Sugar: 1.2mg | |Dietary Fiber: 10.7g| Sodium: 918 mg | Cholesterol: 5mg | Saturated Fat: 1g | Potassium: 1269mg |

Avocado & Black Bean Eggs

Preparation Time: 10 min

Cooking Time: 5 min | Servings: 2

Ingredients

1 small avocado, sliced

2 eggs, beaten

2 tbsps olive oil

1 can of black beans

½ can cherry tomatoes

¼ tsp cumin seeds

Fresh, chopped coriander

1 lime, cut into wedges

2 tsp rapeseed oil

1 red chili

1 clove garlic, sliced

Preparation

1. Heat the olive oil, chili, and garlic in a large skillet and cook until softened. Pour in the beaten eggs and cook until it starts to set.

2. Place the beans and the tomatoes in the pan and add the cumin seeds. Once done, top each serving bowl with avocado and coriander. Serve with lime wedges to enjoy.

Nutritional value

Calories: 625kcal | Carbohydrates: 47g |Protein: 28g |Total Fat: 39g |Sugar: 5mg | Sodium: 0.8mg |Dietary Fiber: 11g| Saturated Fat: 4mg|Cholesterol: 41mg|

Pinto Beans

Preparation Time: 10 min

Cooking Time: 3 hrs | Servings: 8

Ingredients

2 cups dried pinto beans

1 bay leaf

2 large cloves garlic, whole

1 large jalapeño chile pepper, top cut off

4–5 slivers of white onion

1 tbsp sea salt

6 cups water

Preparation

1. Put all the ingredients in a large pot, and bring to a boil.

2. Lower the heat, and simmer for 2 to 3 hours. Check and stir every 30 to 40 minutes, adding water if necessary.

3. Once done, serve to enjoy.

Nutritional value

Calories: 63 kcal | Carbohydrates: 12g |Protein: 4g |Total Fat: 0.3g |Sugar: 0.1mg | Sodium: 543mg |Dietary Fiber: 4g| Saturated Fat: 0.1mg|Cholesterol: 0mg| Potassium: 216mg|

Brazilian Sausage & Black Beans

Preparation Time: 10 min

Cooking Time: 40 min | Servings: 2

Ingredients

1 can (15 ounces.) of black beans

2 tsp vegetable oil

8 oz. low-fat polish kielbasa sausage, cut into small pieces

1 large onion, chopped

1 clove garlic, minced, or ⅛ tsp. garlic powder

1 red bell pepper, chopped

1 tsp ground cumin

1 cup uncooked brown rice

2 cups water

Preparation

1. In a saucepan, heat the vegetable oil over medium-high heat.

2. Saute the onion and sausages in the pan until the onion is tender. Add the garlic, bell pepper, cumin, uncooked rice, black beans,

and water to the saucepan and boil over a high heat setting.

3. Reduce heat and allow to simmer, covered, for 25 to 40 minutes.

Nutritional value

Calories: 485 kcal | Carbohydrates: 45g |Protein: 18g |Total Fat: 26g |Sugar: 1mg | Sodium: 932mg |Dietary Fiber: 7g| Saturated Fat: 7mg|Cholesterol: 54mg| Potassium: 558mg|

Bean Salad in Balsamic Vinaigrette

Preparation Time: 15 min

Cooking Time: 15 min | Servings: 6

Ingredients

¼ cup olive oil

Crackled ground black pepper

2 tbsps balsamic vinegar

⅓ cup fresh parsley

4 garlic cloves

1 medium red onion, diced

4 lettuce leaves

1/2 cup celery

1 can of low-sodium garbanzo beans

1 can of low-sodium black beans

Preparation

1. For the vinaigrette, combine the balsamic vinegar, parsley, garlic, and pepper in a bowl and mix while adding olive oil. Once evenly mixed, set aside.

2. Add the beans and onion in another bowl, stir in the vinaigrette, and toss together gently to coat evenly. Cover and allow to chill before serving. To enjoy, serve with lettuce and garnish with celery.

Nutritional value

Calories: 209 kcal | Carbohydrates: 11g |Protein: 7g |Total Fat: 18.3g |Sugar: 4mg | Sodium: 174 |Dietary Fiber: 4.8g| Saturated Fat: 2.6mg|Cholesterol: 0mg|

Fried Rice

Preparation Time: 10 min

Cooking Time: 15 min | Servings: 4

Ingredients

2 cups cooked brown rice

1 egg

¼ cup chopped parsley

3 tbsps peanut oil

2 tbsps soy sauce

1 tbsp olive oil

½ cup peas

4 green onions, chopped

2 carrots, chopped

1 cup green bell pepper, chopped

Preparation

1. To prepare the rice, heat the peanut oil in a large pot on medium heat. Stir in the cooked rice and saute until it starts to golden. Add all the vegetables and stir-fry for 5 minutes until they are tender.

2. In another pan, scramble your eggs until cooked, and pour the scrambled egg into the rice. Add soy sauce, parsley, and sesame oil and simmer for a few minutes before serving.

Nutritional value

Calories: 243kcal | Carbohydrates: 31g |Protein: 6g |Total Fat: 4.1g |Sugar: 0mg | Sodium: 541.8mg |Dietary Fiber: 1.5g| Saturated Fat: 0.8mg|Cholesterol: 47mg|

Whole-Grain Pancakes

Preparation Time: 10 min

Cooking Time: 30 min | Servings: 4

Ingredients

1 cup whole-wheat flour

¼ cup rolled oats

2 ¼ cups soy milk

3 large egg whites

¼ cup millet flour

1 tbsp olive oil

½ cup barley flour

2 tbsps flaxseed flour

1 ½ tbsps baking powder

3 tbsps honey

Preparation

1. Get a large bowl and mix all the dry ingredients.

2. Mix honey, oil, soy milk, and beaten egg whites in another bowl. Combine wet ingredients with the dry ones and stir. Leave the batter for 30 minutes in the refrigerator.

3. Place a baking sheet into the oven and heat to 225°F. Place a frying pan on medium heat. Scoop ¼ cup of batter into a pan to make one pancake. Flip and cook until brown.

4. Top pancakes with fresh fruit or powdered sugar, and enjoy.

Nutritional value

Calories: 230 kcal | Carbohydrates: 31g |Protein: 6g |Total Fat: 9g |Sugar: 9mg | Sodium: 168mg |Dietary Fiber: 4g| Saturated Fat: 4.5mg|Cholesterol: 80mg|

Easy Brown Rice Risotto with Lamb

Preparation Time: 5 min

Cooking Time: 5 hrs 10 min | Servings: 8

Ingredients

1 pound boneless lamb roast

2 medium carrots, chopped

¾ cup chopped green sweet pepper

2 ½ cups vegetable juice

1 cup brown rice

1 tsp curry powder

¼ tsp salt

Preparation

1. Coat a large non-stick pan with non-stick cooking spray. Preheat the pan over medium heat. Trim fat from meat and cook meat in the hot skillet until browned.

2. Combine vegetable juice, uncooked brown rice, curry powder, and salt in the slow cooker. Top with carrots and set the meat on the carrots. Cover and cook on a high heat setting for 5 hours.

3. Add sweet pepper, cover, and allow to stand until the sweet pepper is tender.

Nutritional value

Calories: 311 kcal | Carbohydrates: 47g |Protein: 10g |Total Fat: 11g |Sugar: 3mg | Sodium: 376mg |Dietary Fiber: 3g| Saturated Fat: 4mg|Cholesterol: 17mg|

Black Bean and Apple Salsa

Preparation Time: 15 min

Cooking Time: 1 min | Servings: 6

Ingredients

1 can of black beans

¼ cup red onion, chopped

½ medium serrano chile pepper, chopped

Juice of ½ large orange

⅛ tp cracked black pepper

⅛ tsp sea salt

½ large Granny Smith apple, cubed

3 tbsps fresh cilantro

Lime juice

Preparation

1. Mix all the ingredients in a bowl.

2. Cover and chill before serving chicken breast or with baked tortilla chips on top.

Nutritional value

Calories: 388 kcal | Carbohydrates: 20g |Protein: 5g |Total Fat: 0.4g |Sugar: 3mg | Sodium: 50mg |Dietary Fiber: 6g| Saturated Fat: 0.1mg|Cholesterol: 0mg|

Stuffed Chilli Bean Peppers

Preparation Time: 10 min

Cooking Time: 15 min | Servings: 6

Ingredients

4 small green, red, or yellow sweet peppers

1 cup cooked converted rice

1 pound can make chili beans with chili gravy

1 pound can of no-salt-added tomato sauce

⅓ cup finely chopped onion

3-pound Monterey Jack cheese, shredded

Chili powder (optional)

Preparation

1. Slice off the top, deseed the peppers. Chop the sweet peppers and set aside.

2. Toss the rice and the beans into a bowl. Mix well and stuff the peppers with the mixture. Spread the tomato sauce in a slow cooker and toss in peppers and onion.

3. Insert the peppers into the slow cooker to keep the stuffed side up. Cover and cook for 3 ½ hours.

4. Remove the peppers from the cooker and, if required, slice them into two. If needed, sprinkle tomato sauce over the stuffed peppers and drizzle with shredded cheese and chili powder.

Nutritional value

Calories: 340 kcal | Carbohydrates: 4g |Protein: 29g |Total Fat: 0.4g |Sugar: 2mg | Sodium: 345mg |Dietary Fiber: 6g| Saturated Fat: 12mg|Cholesterol: 96mg|

Indian Vegetable and Rice Mix

Preparation Time: 10 min

Cooking Time: 40 min | Servings: 2

Ingredients

1 cup white rice, uncooked

1 can of kidney beans, drained

2 tbsps vegetable oil

1 onion, chopped

1 tsp ginger

½ tsp turmeric

1 large baking potato, peeled and diced

½ tsp. salt

2 ½ cups water

½ tsp cumin powder

2 cups mixed vegetables, chopped

Preparation

1. Pour the oil into a skillet and leave on medium heat. Toss in the onion, ginger, and spices and mix well. Leave the mixture for 1-2 minutes to cook, and add the balanced ingredients.

2. Allow the mixture to boil, cover it with a lid and let the mixture simmer for about 25 minutes on reduced heat. Serve immediately.

Nutritional value

Calories: 515 kcal | Carbohydrates: 87g |Protein: 10g |Total Fat: 15g |Sugar: 3mg | Sodium: 905mg |Dietary Fiber: 4g| Saturated Fat: 3mg|

Cheesy Enchiladas

Preparation Time: 10 min

Cooking Time: 30 min | Servings: 6

Ingredients

2 cans black beans, drained and rinsed

8 whole wheat flour tortillas

1 can enchilada sauce

½ cup salsa

1 ½ cups shredded cheese, reduced fat

Preparation

1. Preheat the oven to 350°F. Use oil or cooking spray to grease a 9-inch by 13-inch baking dish. Mix the salsa, beans, half the cheese, and corn in a bowl.

2. Divide the bean mixture among the 8 tortillas. Scoop the mixture into each tortilla and roll the tortillas. Place the tortillas on the baking dish seam side down and pour the enchilada sauce on top.

3. Sprinkle the balance of the cheese over the tortillas and bake in the oven for 20 to 22 minutes.

Nutritional value

Calories: 477 kcal | Carbohydrates: 41.9g |Protein: 5g |Total Fat: 0.4g |Sugar: 8.4mg | Sodium: 50.6mg |Dietary Fiber: 5.5g| Saturated Fat: 15.2mg|Cholesterol: 68.6mg|

Black Eyed Pea Salad

Preparation Time: 10 min

Cooking Time: 10 min | Servings: 6

Ingredients

2 cans of black-eyed peas or black beans

1 avocado (optional)

1 tbsp canola oil

2 tbsps vinegar or lime juice

1 can corn

1 small bunch of cilantro, or to taste

1 bunch of green onions

3 medium tomatoes

Salt and pepper to taste

Preparation

1. Rinse the corn and black-eyed peas or black beans well and drain. Chop the green onions and cilantro finely. Cut the tomatoes and avocados.
2. Mix the corn, black-eyed peas (or black beans), cilantro, onions, tomatoes, and avocado in a large bowl.
3. Mix the vinegar, lime juice, oil, salt, and pepper in a separate bowl. Pour the vinegar mix over the salad; toss gently. Serve as a snack or with a meal.

Nutritional value

Calories: 208 kcal | Carbohydrates: 23g |Protein: 7g |Total Fat: 10g |Sugar: 2mg | Sodium: 499mg |Dietary Fiber: 6g| Saturated Fat: 1mg|Cholesterol: 0mg|

Bean and Spinach Salad

Preparation Time: 10 min

Cooking Time: 15 min | Servings: 4

Ingredients

1 can black beans, rinsed and drained

1 green onion, thinly sliced

1 tbsp snipped fresh cilantro

1 clove garlic, minced

½ cup snipped dried apricots

½ cup chopped red or yellow sweet pepper

¼ cup apricot nectar

2 tbsps salad oil

4 cups shredded fresh spinach

2 tbsps rice vinegar

1 tsp. soy sauce

1 tsp grated fresh ginger

Preparation

1. Mix the apricots, black beans, sweet pepper, cilantro, green onion, and garlic in a medium bowl. Mix the oil, vinegar, apricot nectar, soy sauce, and ginger in a screw-top jar, cover, and shake well.
2. Pour the apricot nectar mix over the bean mixture and toss. Then, cover the bowl and refrigerate for at least 3 hours. Before serving, add spinach to the black bean mix and toss well to mix. Season with salt and pepper.

Nutritional value

Calories: 360 kcal | Carbohydrates: 36g |Protein: 18g |Total Fat: 20g | Sodium: 490 mg |Dietary Fiber: 7g| Saturated Fat: 3mg|Cholesterol: 15mg| Saturated Fat: 0.2mg|Cholesterol: 55mg|

Mushroom Tempeh Stroganoff with Brown Rice

Preparation Time: 10 min

Cooking Time: 40 min | Servings: 6

Ingredients

2 cups cooked brown rice

1 tbsp canola oil

1 pound package of wild rice tempeh

½ yellow onion, thinly sliced

2 cloves garlic, chopped

1 tsp toasted sesame oil

1 large Portobello mushroom, stemmed and sliced

1 tbsp. low sodium Worcestershire sauce

1 packet mushroom gravy mix

4 oz. non-fat sour cream

2 Tbsps. chopped parsley

Preparation

1. Put the rice and water in a saucepan and allow to boil for about 20-25 minutes until the grains become soft.

2. Place the oil in a skillet and heat well. Mix in the tempeh strips and saute until brown on both sides. Please take out the browned tempeh and leave it aside.

3. Toss the garlic and onions into the skillet and saute until soft and tender. Mix in sesame oil, mushrooms, and sauce and leave until mushrooms become soft.

4. Add the tempeh back again to the rest of the ingredients. Mix in the gravy mix according to the directions indicated in the package and allow the mixture to become thick in consistency.

5. Pour the sour cream and let the mixture warm for a while. Place the rice in a dish, and top it with stroganoff and parsley.

Nutritional value

Calories: 251 kcal | Carbohydrates: 20g |Protein: 31g |Total Fat: 1g |Sugar: 5mg | Sodium: 232 mg |Dietary Fiber: 9g| Saturated Fat: 0.2mg|Cholesterol: 55mg|

Sauteed Greens with Cannellini Beans

Preparation Time: 10 min

Cooking Time: 15 min | Servings: 6

Ingredients

1 can cannellini beans, rinsed and drained

1 pound mixed greens, coarsely chopped

3 tbsps extra virgin olive oil

½ small red onion, finely chopped

2 large cloves garlic, minced

¼ tsp chile pepper flakes

⅛ tsp sea salt

⅛ tsp cracked black pepper

3 tbsps water or chicken broth

½ tbsp lemon zest

1/4 cup toasted pine nuts

Preparation

1. Heat the oil in a large sauté pan over medium heat, and add the onion. After a minute, add the garlic and chile pepper flakes, and once the garlic becomes fragrant, add the greens, salt, and pepper. Toss frequently to avoid burning.

2. Add the water or broth, and cover with a lid. After about 3 minutes, remove the lid, add the beans, and cook for another 2 minutes to heat the beans through.

3. Serve the dish with the toasted pine nuts.

Nutritional value

Calories: 302 kcal | Carbohydrates: 31g |Protein: 11g |Total Fat: 17g |Sugar: 0.9mg | Sodium: 67mg |Dietary Fiber: 8g| Saturated Fat: 2mg|Cholesterol: 0mg|

Cilantro-Lime Brown Rice

Preparation Time: 10 min

Cooking Time: 40 min | Servings: 4

Ingredients

¾ cup uncooked brown rice

1 ½ cups low-sodium vegetable broth

Juice of 1 lime

1 tbsp chopped fresh cilantro

Preparation

1. In a small pot, bring the rice and broth to a boil.

2. Then, cover the pot, reduce the heat to low, and simmer for 40 minutes or until the liquid is absorbed.

3. Add the lime juice and cilantro when the rice is fully cooked, and stir to mix well.

Nutritional value

Calories: 56 kcal | Carbohydrates: 12g |Protein: 1g |Total Fat: 0.3g |Sugar: 1mg | Sodium: 174 mg |Dietary Fiber: 1g| Saturated Fat: 0.1mg|Cholesterol: 0mg|

Plain and Simple Couscous

Preparation Time: 5 min

Cooking Time: 10 min | Servings: 4

Ingredients

¾ cup uncooked whole-wheat couscous

⅛ tsp cracked black pepper

¾ cup low-sodium vegetable broth

1 tbsp extra virgin olive oil

Preparation

1. Heat a small pot over medium heat, and add the couscous to toast it until lightly browned and fragrant. Toast for about 2 minutes, stirring constantly. Temporarily place the couscous in a bowl.

2. Add the broth to the pot, and bring it to a boil. Then add the couscous, and remove the pot from the heat. Cover, and let sit for 5 minutes. Fluff the couscous with a fork, drizzle with oil, and sprinkle with pepper before serving.

Nutritional value

Calories: 84kcal | Carbohydrates: 11g |Protein: 3g |Total Fat: 4g |Sugar: 3mg | Sodium: 147mg |Dietary Fiber: 0.9g| Saturated Fat: 0.9mg|Cholesterol: 0mg|

DASH Diet Vegetarian Dishes

Here you will find delicious vegetarian recipes that help you take control of your health. Enjoy!

Vegetarian Chilli with Tofu

Preparation Time: 12 min

Cooking Time: 35 min | Servings: 6

Ingredients

16 ounces tofu

1 can of red kidney beans

1 can of black beans

1 tbsp olive oil

1 small yellow onion, chopped

1 tbsp oregano

1 tbsp chopped fresh cilantro

2 cans diced tomatoes

2 tbsps chili powder

Preparation

1. Heat the olive oil in a small pot over medium heat and saute onions for 5 minutes.
2. Add tofu, beans, tomatoes, oregano, and chili powder, and cook for 30 minutes.
3. Add in the cilantro and serve warm.

Nutritional value

Calories: 387.6kcal | Carbohydrates: 46g |Protein: 26g |Total Fat: 6g |Sugar: 10mg | Sodium: 55mg |Dietary Fiber: 16g| Saturated Fat: 1mg|Cholesterol: 0mg|

Grilled Asparagus

Preparation Time: 10 min

Cooking Time: 10 min | Servings: 4

Ingredients

1 pound asparagus

5 tbsps extra virgin olive oil

Grated zest of 1 large lemon

Juice of 1/2 lemon

3 large cloves garlic, minced

¼ tsp sea salt

⅛ tsp cracked black pepper

Preparation

1. Cut off and discard the thick fibrous ends of the asparagus spears. Lay the spears in a large baking dish or rimmed cookie sheets in a single, even layer and drizzle with oil.
2. Roll the spears in the oil to coat them evenly. Add the lemon zest, lemon juice, garlic, salt, and pepper over the top. Roll the spears
3. Again coat all sides with the seasonings. Place on a hot grill, and rotate the spears constantly so they do not burn. Grill for about 2 minutes, and return to marinating pan to serve.

Nutritional value

Calories: 163 kcal | Carbohydrates: 3g |Protein: 1g |Total Fat: 18g |Sugar: 0mg | Sodium: 50mg |Dietary Fiber: 0.9g| Saturated Fat: 3mg|Cholesterol: 0mg| Potassium: 119 mg|

Oil Free White Bean Hummus

Preparation Time: 10 min

Cooking Time: 10 min | Servings: 10

Ingredients

2 cans cannelli beans

2 cloves garlic

Juice of 1 lemon

2 tbsps tahini

½ tsp red pepper flakes

Pinch of Himalayan sea salt

½ tsp ground black pepper

Preparation

1. Firstly, strain off the canning liquid of the beans and set aside. Place the beans, the canning liquid, garlic, tahini, paprika, lemon juice, chili flakes, salt, and pepper in a food processor and blend on low speed until the humus forms a creamy consistency.

2. Pour hummus into a bowl, and garnish with chili flakes, parsley, and cucumber to enjoy.

Nutritional value

Calories: 76kcal | Carbohydrates: 2g |Protein: 1g |Total Fat: 18g |Sugar: 0.1mg | Sodium: 123.5mg |Dietary Fiber: 2g| Saturated Fat: 1mg|Cholesterol: 0mg| Potassium: 36mg|

Vegetarian Pasta Soup

Preparation Time: 10 min
Cooking Time: 20 min | Servings: 6

Ingredients

2 tsp olive oil

6 cloves garlic, minced

1 ½ cups coarsely shredded carrot

1 cup chopped onion

1 cup thinly sliced celery

1 32-ounce. box low-sodium chicken broth

4 cups water

1 1/2 cups dried ditalini pasta

1/4 cup shaved Parmesan cheese

2 tsp snipped fresh parsley

Preparation

1. First, heat the olive oil in a Dutch oven on medium heat. Next, add the garlic to the pan and cook for 15 seconds. Add the shredded carrot, chopped onion, and sliced celery to the pan and cook for a few minutes, occasionally stirring, until tender.

2. Add the water and chicken broth to the pan and bring it to a boil. Add the uncooked pasta and cook for 8 minutes until the pasta is tender.

3. Top each individual serving with Parmesan cheese and parsley when serving.

Nutritional value

Calories: 213 kcal | Carbohydrates: 42g |Protein: 10.2g |Total Fat: 1.4g |Sugar: 13.2mg | Sodium: 598.4mg |Dietary Fiber: 8.4g| Saturated Fat: 0.4mg|Cholesterol: 1.2mg | Potassium: 832 mg|

Asian Lentils and Pasta

Preparation Time: 15 min
Cooking Time: 15 min | Servings: 4

Ingredients

½ cup pasta

½ cup dry lentils, rinsed

1 large onion, chopped

1 can dice tomatoes with juice

2 cloves garlic, minced

3 cups water

½ cup fresh cilantro, chopped

1 tsp ground cumin

1 tsp. turmeric

2 small dry red peppers

Preparation

1. Place all the ingredients excluding the cilantro, in a skillet. Allow the mixture to boil on medium heat for 35 minutes until the pasta becomes soft.

2. Remove the chili peppers from the mixture. Garnish with cilantro and sour cream, and serve.

Nutritional value

Calories: 497kcal | Carbohydrates: 95g |Protein: 15g |Total Fat: 7.8g |Sugar: 11.9mg | Sodium: 740mg |Dietary Fiber: 9.9g| Saturated Fat: 0.9mg|Potassuim: 1049mg|

Slow Cooker Vegetarian Bolognese

Preparation Time: 30 min

Cooking Time: 4 hrs | Servings: 8

Ingredients

1 (28-ounce) can of diced tomatoes

½ cup dry white wine

½ cup low-sodium vegetable broth or water

1 cup chopped onion

½ cup chopped celery

½ cup chopped carrot

3 tbsps extra-virgin olive oil

2 tbsps minced garlic

½ tsp salt

¼ tsp ground pepper

2 (15 ounces) cans of no-salt-added cannellini beans or small white beans

¼ cup heavy cream

1 pound whole-wheat spaghetti

½ cup grated Parmesan cheese

¼ cup chopped fresh basil

Preparation

1. Combine tomatoes, wine, broth (or water), onion, celery, carrot, oil, garlic, Italian seasoning, salt, and pepper in a slow cooker. Continue cooking on high heat for 4 hours or low for 8 hours. Stir in beans and cream at the end of the cooking time. Keep warm.

2. At this time, bring a large pot of water to a boil. Cook spaghetti according to package directions; drain. Divide the spaghetti among

8 bowls. Top with the sauce, Parmesan, and basil.

Nutritional value

Calories: 434 kcal | Carbohydrates: 64.3g |Protein: 15.9g |Total Fat: 18g |Sugar: 6.2g | Sodium: 411mg |Dietary Fiber: 6.6g| Saturated Fat: 3.5mg|Cholesterol: 12.8mg| Potassium: 762mg|

Eggplant and Pasta Ratatouille

Preparation Time: 10 min

Cooking Time: 15 min | Servings: 4

Ingredients

6 cups water

5 cloves garlic, finely chopped

2 medium green bell peppers, chopped

3 small zucchini, cubed

1 pound pasta

3 tbsps. vegetable oil

1 large onion, chopped

1 small eggplant, cubed

3 medium tomatoes, cubed

1 ½ tsp salt

½ tsp. pepper

2 tsp basil

1 cup Swiss cheese, shredded

Preparation

1. Pour the water into a pot and allow it to boil. Insert the pasta into the boiling water and cook for about 10 minutes until tender but firm to bite. Drain the water and leave the pasta aside.

2. Pour the oil into a skillet and heat well. Saute the onion and garlic and leave for 4-5 minutes until soft.

3. Mix in the bell pepper, eggplant, and zucchini and leave for 10 minutes. Toss in the tomatoes and adjust the seasonings.

4. Allow cooking for another 3-4 minutes until the veggies become soft and tender.

5. Serve with pasta and sprinkle Swiss cheese on the surface.

Nutritional value

Calories: 297 kcal | Carbohydrates: 61.9g |Protein: 11g |Total Fat: 1.5g |Sugar: 12.6g | Sodium: 17mg |Dietary Fiber: 8.8g|Cholesterol: 0mg|

Roasted Cauliflower

Preparation Time: 10 min

Cooking Time: 20 min | Servings: 6

Ingredients

4 cups cauliflower florets

4 tbsps extra virgin olive oil

3 large cloves garlic, minced

½ tsp chile pepper flakes

Grated zest of 1 large lemon

⅛ tsp sea salt

⅛ tsp cracked black pepper

3 tbsps chopped fresh basil

Preparation

1. Preheat the oven to 400°F. Remove and discard the stems and core of the cauliflower. Place the cauliflower head in a baking dish.

2. Drizzle with oil, then sprinkle on the garlic, chile pepper flakes, lemon zest, salt, and pepper. Shake the pan so the oil spreads and the ingredients cover the cauliflower.

3. Bake for 15 to 20 minutes, shaking the pan after 10 minutes to prevent the cauliflower

from sticking. Remove from the heat, top with fresh basil, and serve immediately.

Nutritional value

Calories: 150 kcal | Carbohydrates: 6g |Protein: 2.2g |Total Fat: 14g |Sugar: 0.1g | Sodium: 69mg |Dietary Fiber: 3g| Saturated Fat: 2mg|Cholesterol: 0mg| Potassium: 324mg|

Baked Oatmeal

Preparation Time: 10 min

Cooking Time: 35 min | Servings: 4

Ingredients

1 tbsp canola oil

½ cup unsweetened applesauce

⅓ cup brown sugar

Egg substitute equivalent to 2 eggs

3 cups uncooked rolled oats

2 tsp baking powder

1 tsp cinnamon

1 cup skim milk

Preparation

- In a bowl, stir together oil, applesauce, sugar, and egg substitutes. Add dry ingredients and milk. Mix well.

- Spray a baking pan generously with cooking spray. Spoon oatmeal mixture into pan. Bake at 350°F for 30 minutes.

Nutritional value

Calories: 209kcal | Carbohydrates: 34g |Protein: 8g |Total Fat: 4g |Sugar: 6g | Sodium: 166mg |Dietary Fiber: 4g| Saturated Fat: 1mg|Cholesterol: 1mg| Potassium: 235mg|

Grilled Eggplant and Zucchini

Preparation Time: 15 min

Cooking Time: 25 min | Servings: 4

Ingredients

1 large eggplant, sliced into 1/2-inch rounds

2 zucchini, sliced lengthwise

¼ tsp sea salt, divided

⅛ tsp cracked black pepper

¼ tsp dried parsley

¼ tsp dried basil

¼ tsp dried oregano

6 tbsps balsamic vinegar

4 tbsps extra virgin olive oil

Preparation

1. Lay the sliced eggplant on paper towels, and sprinkle each slice with a pinch of salt to pull out excess moisture. After 10 to 15 minutes, pat the slices dry with paper towels.

2. Arrange the eggplant and zucchini on a cookie sheet with the edges on it. Sprinkle pepper and dried herbs over the veggies, and drizzle with vinegar and oil. Grill the veggies on a hot grill or pan for 4 to 6 minutes, flipping halfway through.

3. Remove from the grill or grill pan and serve.

Nutritional value

Calories: 183 kcal | Carbohydrates: 15g |Protein: 2g |Total Fat: 14g |Sugar: 62g | Sodium: 160mg |Dietary Fiber: 5g| Saturated Fat: 2mg|Cholesterol: 0mg| Potassium: 533 mg|

Sesame Hummus

Preparation Time: 15 min

Cooking Time: 15 min | Servings: 4

Ingredients

2 tbsp olive oil

⅓ cup toasted sesame seeds

⅛ tsp crushed red chilies

1 can garbanzo beans

⅛ cup lime, lemon, or orange juice

½ tsp garlic, minced

½ tsp salt

Preparation

1. Preheat the oven to 350°F. Next, place the seeds on a baking tray and bake for 8 – 10 minutes until slightly toasted. Then, place the sesame seeds in a food processor and process them well into a puree.

2. Mix the chilies, beans, juice, minced garlic, and salt. Process until smooth in consistency. Transfer the mixture to a bowl. Cover and leave it for about 1 hour or more for better blending of flavors.

Nutritional value

Calories: 129 kcal | Carbohydrates: 35g |Protein: 10g |Total Fat: 8.5g |Sugar: 2g | Sodium: 269mg |Dietary Fiber: 3g| Saturated Fat: 1.1mg|Cholesterol: 0mg|

Vegetarian Chilli

Preparation Time: 15 min

Cooking Time: 25 min | Servings: 4

Ingredients

3 large cloves garlic, minced

4 small zucchinis, chopped

3 tbsps extra virgin olive oil

½ large red onion, chopped

½ cup chopped red bell pepper

½ cup chopped yellow bell pepper

2 cans of black beans

1 can of kidney beans

1 tbsp chili powder

½ tsp ground cumin

½ tsp dried parsley

½ tsp dried oregano

½ tsp dried basil

⅛ tsp black pepper

⅛ tsp sea salt

1 can garbanzo beans

2 cans of low-sodium diced tomatoes

¾ cup low-sodium vegetable broth

8 tbsps low-fat plain Greek yogurt

1 large avocado, pitted, peeled, and thinly sliced

4 tbsps chopped fresh cilantro

Preparation

1. Heat the olive oil in a large pot on medium-high heat, and add the onion and garlic. Add the zucchini and bell peppers. Saute the vegetables until the onion is translucent.

2. Transfer to a large pot, and add the remaining ingredients. Cook for 4 - 6 hours on low heat.

3. Serve in bowls and top with yogurt, 2 slices of avocado, and cilantro.

Nutritional value

Calories: 257 kcal | Carbohydrates: 35g |Protein: 10g |Total Fat: 10g |Sugar: 5g | Sodium: 426mg |Dietary Fiber: 11g| Saturated Fat: 1mg|Cholesterol: 0.2mg| Potassium: 851mg|

Kale Vegetable Soup

Preparation Time: 10 min

Cooking Time: 15 min | Servings: 4

Ingredients

2 tbsps extra virgin olive oil

3 medium carrots, sliced

1-quart low-sodium vegetable broth

1 can low-sodium diced tomatoes

3 small sweet potatoes, diced

1 large yellow onion, chopped

3 large cloves garlic, minced

2 small yellow zucchini, cubed

½ tsp dried oregano

¼ tsp chile pepper flakes

⅛ tsp sea salt

1/2 teaspoon fresh thyme, chopped

2 cups coarsely chopped kale

1 can cannellini beans, rinsed and drained

Preparation

1. Heat the olive oil in a large pot on medium heat. Add the carrots, sweet potatoes, onion, and garlic, and cook until they soften, about 4 to 5 minutes. Add the zucchini, oregano, chile pepper flakes, and salt, and cook for 1 minute. Stir in the broth, canned tomatoes with juice, and thyme, and boil.

2. Then decrease heat, cover, and simmer for an additional 10 minutes. Then add the kale and beans, and continue simmering until the kale is wilted and the sweet potatoes are soft for 8 to 10 more minutes. Serve hot.

Nutritional value

Calories: 195 kcal | Carbohydrates: 35g |Protein: 6g |Total Fat: 5g |Sugar: 5g | Sodium: 297mg |Dietary Fiber: 7g| Saturated Fat: 1mg|Cholesterol: 0.2mg| Potassium: 613 mg|

Roasted Almond with Rosemary

Preparation Time: 10 min

Cooking Time: 15 min | Servings: 2

Ingredients

1 bag of whole almonds

1 tbsp fresh rosemary

1 tbsp extra-virgin olive oil

1 tsp chile powder

¾ tsp kosher salt

Dash of ground red pepper

Preparation

1. Preheat the oven to 325°F. Mix all the ingredients in a bowl. Spread the mixture on a lined baking sheet.

2. Bake for about 20-25 minutes until slightly toasted. Leave to cool at room temperature.

Nutritional value

Calories: 111 kcal | Carbohydrates: 3.6g |Protein: 6g |Total Fat: 9.9g |Sugar: 5g | Sodium: 94mg |Dietary Fiber: 2.1g| Saturated Fat: 1mg|Cholesterol: 0.2mg|

Sauteed Vegetables

Preparation Time: 10 min

Cooking Time: 15 min | Servings: 2

Ingredients

1 pound asparagus

1 large green zucchini, sliced

1 large yellow zucchini, sliced

2 tbsps extra virgin olive oil

¼ white onion, chopped

1 large clove of garlic, chopped

1 tablespoon chopped fresh parsley

Juice of 1/2 lemon

⅛ tsp sea salt

⅛ tsp cracked black pepper

Preparation

1. Cut off the tough ends of the asparagus spears.

2. Heat the olive oil in a pan, then add the onion and garlic. After about a minute, add the asparagus.

3. Add the zucchini, parsley, and lemon juice. Cook for 5 more minutes, and then remove from the heat. Season with salt and pepper.

Nutritional value

Calories: 108 kcal | Carbohydrates: 12g |Protein: 3g |Total Fat: 7g |Sugar: 2g | Sodium: 6mg |Dietary Fiber: 4g| Saturated Fat: 1mg|Cholesterol: 0.2mg|

Swiss Apple Panini

Preparation Time: 10 min

Cooking Time: 15 min | Servings: 4

Ingredients

8 slices whole-grain bread

¼ cup non-fat honey mustard

2 crisp apples, thinly sliced

6-pound low-fat Swiss cheese, thinly sliced

1 cup arugula leaves

Preparation

1. Preheat your Panini press or non-stick skillet on medium heat. Spread a light coat of honey mustard over each slice of bread evenly.

2. Layer 4 slices of bread with the cheese, pieces of apple, and arugula leaves. Top each of these slices of bread with the remaining slices of bread.

3. Coat your Panini press lightly with cooking spray. Grill sandwiches till the cheese melts and the bread has toasted.

4. Remove the sandwiches from the skillet. Serve to enjoy.

Nutritional value

Calories: 261 kcal | Carbohydrates: 39g |Protein: 9.7g |Total Fat: 6g | Sodium: 94mg |Dietary Fiber: 4.4g| Saturated Fat: 2mg|Cholesterol: 19mg|

Quinoa and Veggies

Preparation Time: 10 min

Cooking Time: 30 min | Servings: 4

Ingredients

1 cup uncooked quinoa

2 cups vegetable broth

2 tbsps extra virgin olive oil

1/4 cup chopped red onion

1 small clove of garlic, minced

1 large zucchini, chopped into small cubes

⅛ tsp chile pepper flakes

3 cups spinach

Preparation

1. Rinse the quinoa, place it alongside the broth in a large pot, and bring it to a boil. Reduce heat to low, and cover with lid slightly ajar. Simmer on low heat for 15 - 20 minutes or until the liquid is absorbed and the quinoa is uncoiled and tender.

2. Heat the oil in a separate pan over medium heat. Add the onion, garlic, and zucchini, and cook until the onion is translucent. Season with chile flakes, and transfer the veggies to the pot with the cooked quinoa. Add the spinach, stir, and cover the pot.

3. Let sit for 5 minutes. Serve warm.

Nutritional value

Calories: 265 kcal | Carbohydrates: 37g |Protein: 8g |Total Fat: 10g | Sodium: 251mg

|Dietary Fiber: 5g| Saturated Fat: 1mg|Cholesterol: 19mg| Sugar: 5g|

Cherry Mushroom and Spinach Wrap

Preparation Time: 5 min

Cooking Time: 10 min | Servings: 4

Ingredients

1 tbsp. olive oil

8 pounds fresh mushrooms, sliced

1 tsp minced garlic

2 whole wheat 8 inches tortillas

½ pound fresh spinach

1 plum tomato, diced

Preparation

1. Preheat the oven to 350°F. In a sauté pan, heat a tbsp of olive oil over high heat. Add a layer of garlic and mushroom and allow to saute.

2. Arrange the spinach layers over each tortilla, and add the cooked mushrooms, tomato, and mozzarella. Roll up the tortillas.

3. Slightly oil a baking dish and place the tortillas seam-side down. Bake until the cheese melts.

4. Cut the tortillas into quarters crosswise. Serve while warm to enjoy.

Nutritional value

Calories: 139 kcal | Carbohydrates: 10g |Protein: 4g |Total Fat: 10g | Sodium: 651mg |Dietary Fiber: 3g| Saturated Fat: 1mg| Sugar: 5g|

DASH Diet Desserts

Here you will find fun, easy and delicious desserts to satisfy your cravings and boost your health. Enjoy.

Fruit and Nut Bar

Preparation Time: 5 min

Cooking Time: 25 min | Servings: 24

Ingredients

¼ cup honey

¼ cup chopped dried pineapple

2 tbsps cornstarch

½ cup quinoa flour

½ cup oats

¼ cup flaxseed flour

¼ cup wheat germ

¼ cup chopped almonds

5 apricot halves

¼ cup chopped dried figs (about 5 figs)

Preparation

1. Line a sheet pan with parchment. Combine all ingredients, and mix well.

2. Press the mixture into the pan to a thickness of half an inch. Bake at 300 F for 20 minutes. Cool completely and cut into 24 pieces.

Nutritional value

Calories: 70kcal | Carbohydrates: 11g |Protein: 2g |Total Fat: 2g |Sugar: 6mg | Sodium: 4mg |Dietary Fiber: 2g| Saturated Fat: Trace |Cholesterol: 0mg|

Cinnamon and Almond Rice Pudding

Preparation Time: 30 min

Cooking Time: 40 min | Servings: 8

Ingredients

3 cups milk

1 cup white rice

¼ cup sugar

1 tsp. vanilla

¼ tsp almond extract

½ tsp cinnamon to taste

¼ cup toasted almonds (optional)

Preparation

1. In a medium saucepan, combine the milk and rice, and bring it to a boil. Afterward, lower the heat and leave to simmer for 30 minutes until the rice is soft.

2. Once done, remove the pan from the heat, and add the almond extract, cinnamon, vanilla, and sugar. Serve warm, and garnish with toasted almonds on top.

Nutritional value

Calories: 189 kcal | Carbohydrates: 34g |Protein: 2g |Total Fat: 4g |Sugar: 22mg | Sodium: 45mg |Dietary Fiber: 2g| Saturated Fat: 3mg|Cholesterol: 10mg|

Stuffed and Baked Apples

Preparation Time: 10 min

Cooking Time: 40 min | Servings: 4

Ingredients

4 Jonagold baking apples

¼ cup flaked coconut

¼ cup chopped dried apricots

½ cup orange juice

2 tbsps brown sugar

2 tsp grated orange zest

Preparation

1. Peel the top of the apples. Use a knife to hollow out the center of the apples. Place the apples, peeled side up, in a microwave-safe baking dish.
2. Combine the coconut flakes, apricots, and orange zest in a bowl, and mix evenly. Divide the mixture evenly and fill the centers of the apples.
3. In another bowl, mix the brown sugar and orange juice. Pour it over the apples and cover the dish tightly with plastic wrap.
4. Microwave on a high setting until the apples are tender. Serve once cooled to enjoy.

Nutritional value

Calories: 157 kcal | Carbohydrates: 28.4g |Protein: 2.3g |Total Fat: 3g |Sugar: 18.7mg | Sodium: 5.3mg |Dietary Fiber: 3.8g|Calcium: 40.5mg|

Baked Blueberry Bling

Preparation Time: 5 min
Cooking Time: 30 min | Servings: 8

Ingredients

1 tbsp all-purpose flour
1 tbsp brown sugar
½ cup rolled oats
3 cups fresh or frozen blueberries
2 tsp low-salted butter
½ tsp cinnamon

Preparation

1. Preheat oven to 375°F. Prep your blueberries by washing and draining the liquid. Set the blueberries on a pie plate. Mix the flour, butter, oats, sugar, and cinnamon in a small bowl.

2. Pour the oat mixture over the blueberries and bake for 25 minutes. Serve and enjoy while hot.

Nutritional value

Calories: 140kcal | Carbohydrates: 28g |Protein: 3g |Total Fat: 3g |Sugar: 15mg | Sodium: 25mg |Dietary Fiber: 4g| Saturated Fat: 0.5g |Cholesterol: 0mg|

Sweet Carrot and Apple Salad

Preparation Time: 10 min
Cooking Time: 10 min | Servings: 4

Ingredients

2 large Granny Smith apples, cut into matchsticks (about 1 ½ cups)
2 large carrots
1 cup low-fat plain Greek yogurt
¼ cup raisins
1 tsp ground cinnamon
¼ tsp ground ginger
¼ tsp curry powder

Preparation

1. Mix the apples and carrots into the yogurt, and stir in the remaining ingredients.
2. Leave for at least 30 minutes before serving.

Nutritional value

Calories: 117 kcal | Carbohydrates: 41g |Protein: 6g |Total Fat: 0.7g |Sugar: 19mg | Sodium: 50mg |Dietary Fiber: 4g| Saturated Fat: 0g |Cholesterol: 0mg|

Banana Chocolate Dessert Smoothie

Preparation Time: 10 min
Cooking Time: 10 min | Servings: 2

Ingredients

1 medium frozen banana, chopped

¾ cup unsweetened almond milk

¼ cup water

1 ½ tbsps unsweetened cocoa powder

⅛ tsp ground cinnamon

1 tbsp raw, unsalted almond butter

3 drops almond extract

3–4 ice cubes

Sprig of fresh mint

Preparation

1. Place all ingredients except the mint in a blender, and blend on high for a minute.

2. Garnish with fresh mint.

Nutritional value

Calories: 139kcal | Carbohydrates: 41g |Protein: 3g |Total Fat: 7g |Sugar: 9mg | Sodium: 71mg |Dietary Fiber: 4g| Saturated Fat: 1g |Cholesterol: 0mg|

Apple Crumble Pie

Preparation Time: 10 min

Cooking Time: 50 min | Servings: 6

Ingredients

¾ cup all-purpose flour

1 stick cold butter, in chunks 1/2 cup pecans, chopped

2 ½ pound apples, peeled

½ cup brown sugar

½ cup old-fashioned oats

1 tsp cinnamon

½ cup dried cranberries

¼ cup pure maple syrup

Preparation

1. To prepare the topping, process the sugar, oats, butter, cinnamon, and ¾ cup flour in a blender or food processor until moist clusters are formed. Mix in the chopped pecans.

2. Cut the apple into small cubes and place them in a greased pie pan. Add the maple syrup, cranberries, and ½ tbsp flour in a bowl and mix. Spread the mixture on top.

3. Place the pie on a pan baking sheet with parchment lining and bake at 375°F for 45 minutes.

4. Serve to enjoy.

Nutritional value

Calories: 576kcal | Carbohydrates: 77g |Protein: 5g |Total Fat: 29g |Sugar: 43mg | Sodium: 266mg |Dietary Fiber: 7g| Saturated Fat: 2g |Cholesterol: 76mg|

Mini Banana Split

Preparation Time: 5 min

Cooking Time: 10 min | Servings: 2

Ingredients

3 tbsp dark chocolate chips or chopped dark chocolate

1 cup low-fat frozen yogurt

¼ cup strawberries, chopped

1 large banana, sliced

¼ cup pineapple, chopped

2 tbsp toasted chopped almonds

Preparation

1. Place the chocolate in a small bowl and microwave for 10 seconds. Stir the chocolate, and repeat the process until the chocolate is fully melted.

2. Assemble banana splits in two small ramekins by arranging banana slices around the edge of each dish and then scooping frozen yogurt into the center, in the middle of the bananas.

Add the toppings, and drizzle each with chocolate.

Nutritional value

Calories: 332kcal | Carbohydrates: 41g |Protein: 6g |Total Fat: 11g |Sugar: 42mg | Sodium: 0.1mg |Dietary Fiber: 7g| Saturated Fat: 5g |Cholesterol: 5mg|

Sweet Potato Dessert

Preparation Time: 10 min
Cooking Time: 20 min | Servings: 1

Ingredients

1 small or 1/2 large sweet potato

½ cup low-fat vanilla yogurt

¼ tsp ground cinnamon

2 tbsps sliced almonds

Preparation

1. Preheat the oven to 400°F. Pierce the sweet potato with a fork in several places, wrap it in foil, and place it on a cookie sheet to catch any juicy drippings. Bake for 30 - 40 minutes or until the sweet potato is soft and squishy.

2. Remove from the oven, unwrap, and place in a bowl. Cut open down the middle, and top with the yogurt, cinnamon, and almonds.

Nutritional value

Calories: 179kcal | Carbohydrates: 23g |Protein: 9g |Total Fat: 6g |Sugar: 14mg | Sodium: 108mg |Dietary Fiber: 3g| Saturated Fat: 7g |Cholesterol: 7mg|

Spiced Applesauce

Preparation Time: 10 min
Cooking Time: 20 min | Servings: 4

Ingredients

5 large apples, peeled

¼ cup water

1 cinnamon stick

3 cloves

Zest of ½ lemon

½ tsp ground ginger

Preparation

1. Cut the peeled apples into wedges, and discard the cores. Place the apples, water, and spices in a large pot. Cover, and simmer on low heat for 20 minutes.

2. Remove the cinnamon stick and cloves, and mash the apples with a potato masher to the desired consistency.

3. Transfer the mixture to a blender for smooth applesauce, and blend in small batches.

4. Top vanilla ice cream with walnuts, or enjoy as is.

Nutritional value

Calories: 157 kcal | Carbohydrates: 41g |Protein: 0.4g |Total Fat: 0.4g |Sugar: 27mg | Sodium: 0.1mg |Dietary Fiber: 7g| Saturated Fat: 2g |Cholesterol: 0mg|

Berry Sundae

Preparation Time: 10 min
Cooking Time: 15 min | Servings: 6

Ingredients

1 ½ cups raspberries

1 ½ tbsps balsamic vinegar

Pinch of cracked black pepper

1 ½ cups coarsely chopped strawberries

1 ½ cups blueberries

1 ½ cups raspberries

1 ½ tbsps balsamic vinegar

Pinch of cracked black pepper

1 ½ tsp grated lemon zest

1 ½ tsp grated orange zest

Juice of ½ orange

½ tsp vanilla extract

3 cups low-fat plain Greek yogurt

6 tbsps sliced toasted almonds

Preparation

1. Place all ingredients except the yogurt and almonds in a large pot on medium heat, and cook until the liquid bubbles. Decrease the heat to low, and boil the mixture for about 15 minutes or until it thickens. For a smoother sauce, crush the berries with a fork or masher.

2. Remove from the heat. Place ½ cup of yogurt into serving bowls, and top with sauce and toasted almonds.

Nutritional value

Calories: 163 kcal | Carbohydrates: 20g |Protein: 14g |Total Fat: 4g |Sugar: 7mg | Sodium: 47mg |Dietary Fiber: 5g| Saturated Fat: 2g |Cholesterol: 5mg|

Grilled Apricot with Cinnamon

Preparation Time: 5 min

Cooking Time: 5 min | Servings: 4

Ingredients

4 large apricots, halved and pitted

1 tbsp extra virgin olive oil

¼ tsp ground cinnamon

Preparation

1. Brush both sides of each apricot half with oil, and place flat side down on a heated grill or grill pan. Grill for about 4 minutes, turn the apricot halves over and cook for a few more minutes until soft.

2. Remove the apricots from the grill, and sprinkle them with cinnamon. Enjoy warm or chilled.

Nutritional value

Calories: 47kcal | Carbohydrates: 4g |Protein: 5g |Total Fat: 4g |Sugar: 3mg | Sodium: 0.4mg |Dietary Fiber: 0.8g| Saturated Fat: 0.5g |Cholesterol: 0mg|

Strawberries and Cream Cheese Crepes

Preparation Time: 15 min

Cooking Time: 20 min | Servings: 4

Ingredients

2 tsp vanilla extract

2 prepackaged crepes

8 strawberries, sliced

1 tsp powdered sugar

2 tsp caramel sauce

4 tbsps cream cheese

Preparation

1. Heat the oven to 325°F.

2. Use an electric mixer and blend the cream cheese in a mixing bowl until smooth. Add the powdered sugar and vanilla and combine well.

3. Spread the cream cheese mixture on each crepe and top with 2 tbsps of strawberries. Roll up and place in an already sprayed baking dish. Bake for 10 minutes until golden brown.

4. Cut crepes in half and transfer to serving plates. Sprinkle with powdered sugar and caramel sauce to enjoy.

Nutritional value

Calories: 150kcal | Carbohydrates: 20g |Protein: 6g |Total Fat: 5g |Sugar: 9mg |

Sodium: 161mg |Dietary Fiber: 1g| Saturated Fat: 4mg|Cholesterol: 46mg|

Cucumber-Watermelon Cooler

Preparation Time: 5 min

Cooking Time: 5 min | Servings: 4

Ingredients

5 cups chopped seedless watermelon

1 cup chopped unpeeled cucumber

10 fresh mint leaves

Juice of 1/2 lime

Preparation

1. Blend the watermelon and cucumber in the blender. Add the mint and lime juice to the last blend. Serve chilled as a beverage or summer soup, or freeze in Popsicle molds for a light treat.

Nutritional value

Calories: 66 kcal | Carbohydrates: 15g |Protein: 2g |Total Fat: 0.9g |Sugar: 15mg | Sodium: 5mg |Dietary Fiber: 4g| Saturated Fat: 0.1g |Cholesterol: 0mg|

Grilled Pineapple

Preparation Time: 5 min

Cooking Time: 5 min | Servings: 6

Ingredients

1 large pineapple, sliced into rounds and cored

Preparation

1. Cut the pineapple by laying it on its side and cutting off the top and bottom. In a circular motion, cut the skin off, starting from the top and going to the base. Once the skin has been removed, slice rounds to desired thickness.

2. Place the pineapple rings directly onto a hot grill. Next, grill for 3 minutes or until char

marks appear. Then turn the rings over and grill for another 2 to 3 minutes. Serve warm or chilled.

Nutritional value

Calories: 39kcal | Carbohydrates: 10g |Protein: 0.3g |Total Fat: 0.4g |Sugar: 8mg | Sodium: 0.8mg |Dietary Fiber: 1g|Cholesterol: 0mg|

Creamy Fruit Dessert

Preparation Time: 10 min

Cooking Time: 10 min | Servings: 4

Ingredients

4 ounces of fat-free cream cheese, softened

1 can (15 ounces) mandarin oranges, drained

1 can (14.5 ounces) water-packed sliced peaches, drained

1 can (8 ounces) water-packed pineapple chunks, drained

4 tbsps shredded coconut, toasted

½ cup plain fat-free yogurt

1 tsp sugar

½ tsp vanilla extract

Preparation

1. Combine the cream cheese, yogurt, sugar, and vanilla in a small bowl. Then use a mixer to beat until smooth.

2. Drain the canned fruit. In a separate bowl, combine the oranges, peaches, and pineapple. Add the cream cheese mixture and fold it together. Cover and refrigerate until well-chilled.

3. Transfer to a serving bowl or individual bowls. Garnish with shredded coconut and serve immediately.

Nutritional value

Calories: 206 kcal | Carbohydrates: 41g |Protein: 6g |Total Fat: 2g |Sugar: 38mg | Sodium: 241 mg |Dietary Fiber: 2g| Saturated Fat: 1.5mg|Cholesterol: 3mg|

Mixed Berry Pie

Preparation Time: 10 min

Cooking Time: 10 min | Servings: 4

Ingredients

½ cup fat-free, sugar-free instant vanilla pudding made with fat-free milk

¾ cup sliced strawberries (about 12 to 15 medium strawberries)

6 single-serve (tart-size) graham cracker pie crusts

6 tbsps light whipped topping

¾ cup raspberries

6 mint leaves for garnish

Preparation

1. Make pudding according to the directions on the package.
2. In a small bowl, mix the strawberries and raspberries.
3. Divide the pudding among the pie crusts (about 4 teaspoons each). Add about 2 tablespoons of the berry mix to each pie. Top each with 1 tablespoon of whipped topping. Garnish with mint leaves.
4. Serve and enjoy!

Nutritional value

Calories: 133 kcal | Carbohydrates: 20g |Protein: 2g |Total Fat: 5g |Sugar: 8mg | Sodium: 169 mg |Dietary Fiber: 2g| Saturated Fat: 3g |Cholesterol: 0.5|

Vanilla Poached Peaches

Preparation Time: 15 min

Cooking Time: 20 min | Servings: 6

Ingredients

6 medium size ripe peaches

2 cups water

Mint leaf

½ cup granulated sugar

1 vanilla bean

Preparation

1. First, scrape the vanilla bean and set aside the scrapings. Add the water, sugar, vanilla bean, and scrapings in a large saucepan and stir on low heat until the sugar dissolves. Simmer the mixture for 10 minutes until you notice it is thickening.
2. Cut up the ripe peaches, and add the cut fruit into the mix. Poach on low heat for 5 minutes. Once done, transfer the peaches and sauce to your serving bowls.
3. Garnish with mint leaves if desired, and enjoy immediately.

Nutritional value

Calories: 156 kcal | Carbohydrates: 38g |Protein: 1g |Total Fat: Trace |Sugar: 24mg | Sodium: 2mg |Dietary Fiber: 2g| Saturated Fat: 3g |Cholesterol: 0.5|

Sweet Potato and Squash Pie

Preparation Time: 10 min

Cooking Time: 1 hr | Servings: 8

Ingredients

1 cup mashed sweet potato

1 tsp orange zest

3 tbsps honey

1 butternut squash

½ cup silken tofu

½ cup milk

4 eggs

¼ cup rye flour

½ tsp allspice

½ tsp vanilla extract

1 tsp freshly grated ginger

1 9-inch pie crust

Preparation

- Heat oven to 300°F. Boil and mash the sweet potato and squash in a food processor. Set the mixture in a bowl and add the remaining ingredients. Combine until smooth.

- Pour the mixture into a pie crust on a sheet pan and bake for 55 minutes. Once cooled, serve to enjoy.

Nutritional value

Calories: 399 kcal | Carbohydrates: 34g |Protein: 5g |Total Fat: 12g |Sugar: 7mg | Sodium: 109mg |Dietary Fiber: 4g| Saturated Fat: 4g |Cholesterol: 0mg|

DASH Diet Nutritious Drinks

There are many healthier options for your drinks and beverages. Here is a selection of options to quench your thirst.

Watermelon Aguas Frescas

Ingredients

4 cups cubed watermelon

1 tbsp sugar, honey, or agave nectar

3 cups water

3 tsp fresh lime juice

Fresh mint for garnish

Preparation

1. Put the cubed watermelon in a blender and add 1 ½ cups of water, lime juice, and sugar. Blend at high speed until smooth.
2. Use a medium strainer to sieve the liquid blend into a large pitcher.
3. Add the remaining water and stir.
4. Garnish with fresh mint if you desire.

Nutritional Value

Calories: 57kcal | Sodium: 1mg | Carbohydrates: 14g |Protein: 1g | Total fat: 0g | Sugar: 17g | Calcium: 8mg | Potassium: 90mg

Blueberry Green Smoothie

Ingredients

2 cups chopped greens (such as kale, collard greens, mustard greens, Swiss chard, and spinach)

¼ cup water

⅓ cup chopped carrot

½ cup frozen blueberries

½ cup coarsely chopped unpeeled cucumber

¼ cup unsweetened almond milk

4 ice cubes

Preparation

1. Place the greens and water in a blender. Start blending on low, and as the greens break down, increase to medium speed until they are completely broken down and smooth.
2. Add the remaining ingredients, and blend on medium to high speed until desired consistency for 1 minute. Serve immediately.

Nutritional Value

Calories: 82kcal | Carbohydrates: 17g |Protein: 4g | Total fat: 1g | Sodium: 66mg| Potassium: 516mg| Sugar: 7g|

Banana and Spinach Smoothie

Ingredients

1 medium banana

½ cup fat-free milk

¼ cup whole oats

¾ cup frozen mango

¼ cup plain non-fat yogurt

1 baby spinach

½ tsp vanilla

Preparation

1. Place the oats in a blender, pour the milk and yogurt, and blend for 16 seconds.
2. Toss in the mango, spinach, banana, and vanilla, and mix until the mixture is smooth.

Nutritional Value

Calories: 257kcal | Carbohydrates: 47g |Sugar: 26mg | Sodium: 143mg | Dietary Fiber: | Protein: 10g| Total Fat: 5g| Saturated Fat: 1g|Calcuim: 90mg|

Orange Creamsicle Smoothie

Ingredients

1 small orange

1 cantaloupe, chopped

I tsp vanilla

½ frozen banana

6 ice cubes

Preparation

1. Combine all the fruits and ice cubes in a blender until smooth.
2. Pour into a glass and enjoy chilled.

Nutritional Value

Calories: 176kcal | Carbohydrates: 43g |Protein: 13g |Total Fat: 9g |Sugar: 1g | Dietary Fiber: 6g| Saturated Fat: 1g | Sodium: 19mg|

Berry Banana Green Smoothie

Ingredients

2 cups spinach

¾ cup frozen blueberries

1 small frozen banana, chopped

1 cup water

¾ cup frozen blackberries

1 tbsp almond butter

Preparation

1. Add the spinach and water to a blender and blend on low until smooth.
2. Add the blackberries, blueberries, banana, and almond butter, and mix until desired consistency is achieved.

Nutritional Value

Calories: 159kcal | Carbohydrates: 29g | Sodium: 30mg |Total Fat: 5g | Cholesterol: 0mg |Dietary Fiber: 7g |Sugar: 13 |Protein: 4g |

Papaya Goodness

Ingredients

1 cup spinach

1 cup chopped kale

¾ cup water

½ cup chopped unpeeled cucumber

1 green apple, coarsely chopped

1 cup coarsely chopped papaya

1 tbsp ground flaxseed

Preparation

1. Place the spinach, kale, and water in a blender. Start blending on low, and as the greens break down, increase to medium speed until they are completely broken down and smooth.
2. Add the remaining ingredients, and blend medium to high speed for 1 minute until desired consistency. Serve immediately.

Nutritional Value

Calories: 114kcal | Carbohydrates: 25g |Protein: 3g | Total fat: 2g | Sodium: 32mg| Potassium: 520mg| Sugar: 14g|

Banana Almond Smoothie

Ingredients

1 large banana

1 cup unsweetened almond milk

1 tablespoon unsalted almond butter

1 tablespoon wheat germ

1/8 teaspoon vanilla extract

1/8 teaspoon ground cinnamon

3–4 ice cubes

Preparation

1. Place all the ingredients in a blender. Start blending on low, and as the contents break

down, increase to medium speed until desired consistency.

2. Serve immediately.

Nutritional Value

Calories: 338kcal | Carbohydrates: 52g |Protein: 10g | Total fat: 13g | Sodium: 153mg| Potassium: 857mg| Sugar: 25g|

Melon Melange

Ingredients

2 cups spinach

½ –¾ cup water

½ cup frozen strawberries

¾ cup chopped honeydew melon

¾ cup chopped cantaloupe

1 tbsp ground flaxseeds

3–4 ice cubes

Preparation

1. Place the spinach and water in a blender. Start blending on low, and as the spinach begins to break down, increase to medium speed until it is completely broken down and smooth.

2. Add the fruit, flaxseeds, and ice, and blend on medium to high speed until desired consistency.

3. Serve immediately.

Nutritional Value

Calories: 77kcal | Carbohydrates: 52g |Protein: 3g | Total fat: 2g | Sodium: 43mg| Potassium: 376mg| Sugar: 7g|

Mango Raspberry Sorbet

Ingredients

½ cup frozen mango

½ cup Orange Juice (Unsweetened)

½ cup frozen raspberries

Preparation

1. Place frozen raspberries and frozen mangos in a blender. Pour unsweetened Orange Juice over the mix.

2. Blend on high speed until smooth. Place in a serving cup with a mint sprig if desired, and enjoy.

Nutritional Value

Calories: 144kcal | Carbohydrates: 34g |Protein: 2g |Sugar: 12mg | Sodium: 4mg |Dietary Fiber: 5g|

Arugula Smoothie

Ingredients

1 cup arugula

1 cup spinach

1 – 1 ½ cups water

½ small banana

1 cup chopped strawberries

½ cup blueberries

1 tbsp coconut oil

1 tbsp wheat germ

3–4 ice cubes

Preparation

1. Place the arugula, spinach, and water in a blender. Start blending on low, and as the greens break down, increase to medium speed until they are completely broken down and smooth.

2. Add the fruit, coconut oil, wheat germ, and ice, and blend on medium to high speed until desired consistency, for 1 minute.

3. Serve immediately.

Nutritional Value

Calories: 154kcal | Carbohydrates: 21g |Protein: 3g |Sugar: 11mg | Sodium: 19mg

|Dietary Fiber: 5g| Total fat: 8g| Potassium: 437mg|

Pumpkin Pie Smoothie

Ingredients

½ cup pumpkin puree

½ large frozen banana, chopped

½ cup water

1 cup unsweetened almond milk

¼ tsp ground cinnamon

⅛ tsp ground nutmeg

1 tbsp pure maple syrup

3–4 ice cubes

Preparation

1. Place the pumpkin, banana, and water in a blender. Start blending on low, and as the ingredients break down, increase to medium speed until completely broken down and smooth.

2. Add the remaining ingredients, and blend on medium to high speed until desired consistency for 1 minute.

3. Serve immediately.

Nutritional Value

Calories: 93kcal | Carbohydrates: 19g |Protein: 3g |Sugar: 10mg | Sodium: 93mg |Dietary Fiber: 2g| Total fat: 2g| Potassium: 394mg|

Strawberry Cucumber Delight

Ingredients

1 ½ cups frozen strawberries

2 cups chopped unpeeled cucumber

Juice of ½ large orange

4 mint leaves

¾ cup water

3–4 ice cubes

Preparation

1. Place all the ingredients in a blender. Start blending on low, and as the contents break down, increase to medium speed until desired consistency for 1 minute.

2. Serve immediately.

Nutritional Value

Calories: 61kcal | Carbohydrates: 14g |Protein: Trace |Sugar: 9mg | Sodium: 4mg |Dietary Fiber: 4g| Total fat: 0.7g|

Green Avocado Smoothie

Ingredients

1 cup chopped kale

¾ -1 cup water

1 green apple

2 small kiwi fruits

1 small avocado

1 tangerine

3–4 ice cubes

Preparation

1. Place the kale and water in a blender. Start blending on low, and as the kale breaks down, increase to medium speed until completely broken down and smooth.

2. Add the remaining ingredients, and blend on medium to high speed until desired consistency, for 1 minute.

3. Serve immediately.

Nutritional Value

Calories: 271kcal | Carbohydrates: 39g |Protein: 4g |Sugar: 10mg | Sodium: 29mg |Dietary Fiber: 13g| Total fat: 15g| Potassium: 916mg|

Chocolate Smoothie with Avocado and Banana

Ingredients

2 cups vanilla soy milk

½ avocado, pitted and peeled

1 medium banana, peeled

¼ cup unsweetened cocoa powder

Preparation

1. Put all ingredients in a blender and process until smooth.

2. Serve immediately to enjoy.

Nutritional Value

Calories: 252kcal | Carbohydrates: 33g |Protein: 11g |Sugar: 8mg | Sodium: 102mg |Dietary Fiber: 8g| Total fat: 12g| Potassium: 822mg|

Hurricane Punch

Ingredients

1 ½ cups chopped pineapple

2 cups citrus fruit

Juice of 1 lemon (about 2 tablespoons)

8 ounces cranberry juice

1 cup ice plus extra for serving

Preparation

1. Put all ingredients except ice in a blender and puree until very smooth. Add 1 cup ice and puree until smooth. Serve over ice if desired.

2. Garnish with slices of orange or chunks of pineapple.

Nutritional Value

Calories: 64kcal | Carbohydrates: 15g |Sugar: 12mg | Sodium: 6mg |Total Fat: 0g Cholesterol: 0mg |Dietary Fiber: 2g |Protein: 1g|

Melon & Orange Slushy

Ingredients

5 ice cubes, slightly crushed

4 cups cubed ripe cantaloupe

¼ cup fresh orange juice

Preparation

1. Add the melon, orange juice, and crushed ice in a blender. Blend until it is smooth but slushy.

2. Serve the slushy immediately, while cool, with slices of lemon.

Nutritional Value

Calories: 147kcal | Carbohydrates: 36g |Sugar: 29mg | Sodium: 8mg |Total Fat: 1g Calcium: 35mg |Dietary Fiber: 1g |Protein: 3g|

Iced Latte

Ingredients

2 cups brewed decaffeinated espresso coffee, cooled

2 tbsps golden brown sugar

1 ½ cups fat-free milk

2 tbsps sugar-free almond syrup*

Ice cubes

1 cup fat-free whipped topping

1 tsp ground espresso beans

Preparation

1. Combine the espresso, brown sugar, milk, and syrup in a pitcher. Stir to mix evenly. Refrigerate until cold.

2. Fill 4 glasses with ice cubes. Pour coffee over ice. Add ¼ cup whipped topping to each drink and sprinkle with ground espresso beans.

Nutritional Value

Calories: 84kcal | Carbohydrates: 18g |Sugar: 11mg | Sodium: 82mg |Total Fat: Trace|

Cholesterol: 2mg |Dietary Fiber: 0g |Protein: 3g|

Creamy Apple Shake

Ingredients

2 cups vanilla low-fat ice cream

1 cup unsweetened applesauce

¼ tsp ground cinnamon or apple pie spice

1 cup fat-free skim milk

Preparation

1. Combine the ice cream, cinnamon, apple pie spice, and apple sauce in a blender, and cover until smooth.

2. Add the skim milk to the blender, cover, and blend well until mixed.

3. Pour the shake into glasses and sprinkle each serving with more cinnamon if desired.

4. Serve immediately.

Nutritional Value

Calories: 239kcal | Carbohydrates: 38g |Sugar: 35mg | Sodium: 101mg |Total Fat: 7g Cholesterol: 29mg |Dietary Fiber: 2g |Sugar: 35|Protein: 7g|

Island Chiller

Ingredients

2 packages (10 ounces each) of frozen unsweetened strawberries

1 ½ cans (about 30 ounces) of crushed pineapple with juice

3 cups orange juice with pulp

2 quarts carbonated water, chilled

16 fresh strawberries

Preparation

1. In a blender, combine the frozen strawberries and pineapple in a blender with juice and orange juice. Blend until smooth and frothy.

2. Pour the mixture into the ice cube trays and put it in the freezer.

3. To serve, put 3 cubes into a tall glass and fill it with ½ cup of carbonated water. Wait until the mixture becomes slushy.

4. Garnish with a strawberry and serve.

Nutritional Value

Calories: 80kcal | Carbohydrates: 19g |Sugar: 15mg | Sodium: 2mg |Total Fat: 0g |Cholesterol: 0mg |Dietary Fiber: 9g |Protein: 1g|

Fresh Fruit Smoothie

Ingredients

1 cup fresh pineapple chunks

½ cup cantaloupe or other melon chunks

1 cup fresh strawberries

Juice of 2 oranges

1 cup cold water

1 tbsp honey

Preparation

1. Remove the rind from the pineapple and melon. Cut into chunks. Remove stems from strawberries.

2. Put all ingredients into the blender and puree until smooth. Serve cold.

Nutritional Value

Calories: 72kcal | Carbohydrates: 17g |Sugar: 13mg | Sodium: 7mg |Total Fat: 0g |Cholesterol: 0mg |Dietary Fiber: 1g |Protein: 37g|

Non-Alcoholic Margarita

Ingredients
Simple syrup:
½ cup sugar
½ cup water
Margaritas:
2 cups ice
1/2 cup fresh lime juice
3 tbsp simple syrup
Cut fresh fruit to garnish

Preparation
1. In a small saucepan, heat sugar, and water. Stir until sugar is dissolved. Remove from heat and chill.
2. Add ice, juice, and simple syrup. Blend until smooth, pour in your chilled glass, and garnish the rim with cut fruit.

Nutritional Value
Calories: 68kcal | Carbohydrates: 17g |Sugar: 12mg | Sodium: 2mg |Total Fat: 7g | Cholesterol: 0mg |Dietary Fiber: Trace |Protein: Trace|

Watermelon & Lemon Sorbet

Ingredients
8 cups cubed (1 inch) watermelon
2 tbsps fresh lemon juice

Preparation
1. In a blender, puree the watermelon cubes.
2. Place 4 cups of the puree in a medium size bowl.
3. Stir in the lemon juice and freeze it in an ice cream maker.

Nutritional Value

Calories: 116kcal | Carbohydrates: 30g |Sugar: 29g | Sodium: 1mg |Total Fat: 0g |Potassium: 74mg |Dietary Fiber: 0g |Protein: 0g|

Strawberry Banana Milkshake

Ingredients
6 frozen strawberries, chopped
1 medium banana
½ cup soy milk
1 cup fat-free vanilla frozen yogurt
2 fresh strawberries, sliced

Preparation
1. Combine the frozen strawberries, banana, soy milk, and yogurt in a blender. Blend until smooth.
2. Pour into tall, frosty glasses and garnish each with fresh strawberry slices. Serve immediately.

Nutritional Value
Calories: 163kcal | Carbohydrates: 33g |Sugar: 20g | Sodium: 94mg |Total Fat: 1g|Cholesterol: 3mg |Dietary Fiber: 4g |Protein: 6g|

Cookies and Cream Shakes

Ingredients
1 ⅓ cups vanilla soy milk (soya milk), chilled
3 cups fat-free vanilla ice cream
6 chocolate wafer cookies, crushed

Preparation
1. In a blender, combine soy milk and ice cream. Blend until smooth and frothy. Add cookies and pulse a few times to blend.
2. Pour into tall, chilled glasses and serve immediately.

Nutritional Value

Calories: 270 kcal | Carbohydrates: 52g |Sugar: 29g | Sodium: 224 mg |Total Fat: 3g|Cholesterol: Trace |Dietary Fiber: 11.5g |Protein: 9g|

Berry Mix Smoothie

Ingredients

1 ½ cups strawberries

½ cup blueberries

⅓ cup water or ⅓ plain vanilla yogurt

Vanilla extract

1 tbsp flaxseed

Preparation

1. Place all the ingredients in a blender. Process until smooth in consistency.

2. Serve garnished with strawberries if desired.

Nutritional Value

Calories: 154kcal | Carbohydrates: 36g |Sugar: 29g | Sodium: 15mg |Total Fat: 1g|Cholesterol: 1mg |Dietary Fiber: 3g |Protein: 2g|

Green Tea and Cranberry Smoothie

Ingredients

½ cup frozen cranberries

¼ cup frozen blueberries

½ cup frozen blackberries

5 frozen whole strawberries

1 ripe banana

½ cup brewed green tea, cooled to room temperature

¼ cup plain soy milk

2 tbsps honey or packed light brown sugar

Preparation

1. Place the ingredients in a blender. Blend the mixture until smooth in consistency.

Nutritional Value

Calories: 378kcal | Carbohydrates: 31g | Sodium: 38mg |Total Fat: 2g|Cholesterol: 0.0mg |Dietary Fiber: 11g |Protein: 5.2.g|

Peach and Raspberry Parfait

Ingredients

1 cup fresh sliced peaches

1½ cups low-fat or fat-free milk

⅛ tsp almond extract

1 cup fresh raspberries

Preparation

1. Place the peaches, almond extract, and milk in a blender until smooth.

2. Botch the raspberries using a fork.

3. Lay the milk and mashed raspberries in two separate glasses.

Nutritional Value

Calories: 260kcal | Carbohydrates: 45g |Sugar: 23g | Sodium: 105mg |Total Fat: 4g|Cholesterol: 5mg |Dietary Fiber: 4g |Protein: 10g|

Ginger and Mint Tisane

Ingredients

6 cups water

¼ cup peeled and chopped fresh ginger

⅓ cup fresh lemon juice

½ cup firmly packed fresh mint leaves

6 tbsps dark honey

1 lemon, cut into 6 wedges

Preparation

1. Pour the water into a saucepan and leave on high heat. Mix in the fresh ginger and lemon juice and allow to boil. Reduce the heat to low and leave for 5 minutes.

2. Take out from the heat, toss in the mint, and leave for 5-6 minutes. Pour the mixture into a sieve pitched over a jug.

3. Remove the remnants of ginger and mint from the sieve. Add the honey and mix well.

4. The Tisane can be served chilled or hot. Garnish with a lemon wedge when serving.

Nutritional Value

Calories: 62kcal | Carbohydrates: 17g |Sugar: 16g | Sodium: 3mg |Total Fat: 3g|Cholesterol: 0mg |Dietary Fiber: 11.5g | Potassium: 44mg|

Pineapple Cucumber and Kale Juice

Ingredients

1 small pineapple, cleaned

8 leaves of curly kale

½ of English cucumber

1 slice of lemon (optional)

Preparation

1. Slice the pineapple and cut it into chunks. Peel and slice the cucumber lengthwise.

2. Insert the pineapple chunks and kale leaves into a blender. Mix a slice of lemon into the blender. Process until smooth.

3. Extract the juice of the cucumber and mix all ingredients.

Nutritional Value

Calories: 257kcal | Carbohydrates: 41g |Sugar: 25g | Sodium: 36mg |Total Fat: 8g|Cholesterol: Trace |Dietary Fiber: 3g |Protein: 10g|

Part 5

30-Day Meal Plan

The DASH diet eating plan requires no special foods. Instead, it is focused on servings of food groups. To get the true experience of the DASH diet, I have mapped out a simple meal plan for the next month. This meal plan is based on 2000 calories per day for the regular dash diet.

Day 1

Breakfast: 1 egg muffin, ½ grapefruit, coffee with 4 ounces of non-fat milk, or green tea with lemon.

Lunch: 1 serving Broccoli Soup, topped with grated Parmesan cheese, ¼ cup hummus (2 tbsps) with baby carrots and sliced bell pepper, and 1 cup strawberries.

Snack

8 ounces of non-fat plain Greek yogurt with ½ cup blueberries.

Dinner

4 turkey meatballs in Marinara Sauce (3 meatballs), 1 cup steamed spinach with garlic and 1 teaspoon extra virgin olive oil, 1 slice of 100% whole wheat bread, 2 slices pineapple (1 piece), and 6–8 ounces sparkling water.

Day 2

Breakfast: 1 serving of warm quinoa with berries, 1 tbsp sliced almonds, and coffee with 8-ounce non-fat milk or tea.

Lunch: 1 chicken fajita wrap, ½ cup tropical salsa, and 1 medium orange.

Snack: 2-ounce mozzarella cheese, ½ cup grapes.

Dinner: 1 cup pinto beans, 2 fish tacos, ½ cup tropical salsa, and two grilled pineapple slices.

Day 3

Breakfast: 2 eggs scrambled in 1 tbsp butter and ½ cup berries.

Lunch: 1 cup cooked whole grain pasta, ½ cup tomato sauce, ½ cup vegetables, and ½ cup toasted almonds.

Snack: 1-ounce cheese and 4 whole grain crackers.

Dinner: 3-ounce chicken breast, 1 cup sugar snap peas sauteed in 1 tsp olive oil, 1 ½ cups dark green salad, and 1 cup fruit juice.

Day 4

Breakfast: a green blueberry smoothie, 2 slices 100% whole wheat toast with 2 tbsps peanut butter.

Lunch: 1 serving of roasted salmon, 8 ounces of non-fat milk, 1 medium orange.

Snack: 1 cup of cherries and 20 almonds.

Dinner: 1 serving of healthy Italian pasta Salad, 5 ounces grilled or baked boneless, skinless chicken breast, and 1 cup of frozen grapes.

Day 5

Breakfast: 1 tuna Sandwich, 8 ounces of non-fat milk, or coffee with up to 8 ounces of non-fat milk and 1 cup of mixed berries.

Lunch: 1 serving of healthy cobb salad with 1 tablespoon basic vinaigrette, 1 100% whole wheat pita bread, and 1 medium apple

Snack: 1 cup air-popped popcorn with 1 teaspoon butter and 1 medium orange.

Dinner: 1 serving stuffed Bell Pepper, 1 cup steamed broccoli, 1 serving melon melange.

Day 6

Breakfast: 1 serving banana oatmeal pancake, coffee with up to 8 ounces of non-fat milk, 1 slice 100% whole wheat bread, and 1/2 cup grapes.

Lunch: 1 serving Asian Quinoa Salad, ½ cup baby carrots, and 1 medium peach.

Snack: ½ cup of canned peaches and 1 cup of low-fat yogurt.

Dinner: 1 serving of easy lemon-baked fish and 1 serving of mixed berry pie.

Day 7

Breakfast: 1 serving Banana Almond Smoothie, 2 slices of 100% whole wheat bread, and 2 ounces of goat cheese.

Lunch: 1 serving tuna salad with 1 ½ cups spinach, ½ sliced avocado, ½ cup cherry tomatoes, and 1 cup mixed berries.

Snack: 2 multigrain rice cakes and ¼ cup hummus (2 tbsps).

Dinner: 1 serving of Thai curried vegetables, 1 cup brown rice, ½ cup strawberries with 1 tbsp homemade whipped cream.

Day 8

Breakfast: 1 cup steel-cut oatmeal with ½ cup milk and 2 tbsp dried fruit.

Lunch: 2 cups kale salad with 1 tbsp olive oil, balsamic vinegar, ½ cup beans, and ¼ cup toasted pecans.

Snacks: 1 apple and 4 whole grain crackers.

Dinner: 3-ounce beef burger, 3 sweet potato wedges, 1 cup serving orange strawberry twirl.

Day 9

Breakfast: 1 serving tropical smoothie, 1 100% whole wheat English muffin with 2 tbsps peanut butter or almond butter.

Lunch: 1 serving Italian veggie pita sandwich, with 4 ounces grilled or baked boneless, skinless chicken breast, 8 ounces non-fat milk, and ½ cup grapes

Snack: ½ cup plain Greek yogurt and ½ cup dried fruit.

Dinner: 2 grilled chicken skewers marinated in ginger-apricot Sauce, 1 cup brown rice, 1 cup roasted cauliflower, 1 brie-stuffed Apple.

Day 10

Breakfast: 1 slice whole wheat french toast and ½ cup berries.

Lunch: 2 cups cooked whole grain pasta with ½ cup tomato sauce and 1 ½ cups dark green salad.

Snack: ½ cup dried fruit and ½ cup nuts.

Dinner: 3-ounce turkey breast, 1 cup mashed yellow-fleshed potatoes with 1 tbsp olive oil, 6-8 ounces sparkling water.

Day 11

Breakfast: 1 serving fruity yogurt parfait, 1 tbsp almonds, coffee with 4 ounces of non-fat milk.

Lunch: 1 serving of Kale Vegetable Soup, 8 ounces of non-fat milk, 1 toasted cheese sandwich with reduced fat, mozzarella cheese on 1 slice of 100% whole wheat bread.

Snack: ¼ cup hummus dip with Curried Pita Chips, ½ cup grapes.

Dinner: 2 slices of Mexican pizza, 1 serving of beet and heirloom tomato salad, 1 cup of macerated strawberries with homemade whipped cream.

Day 12

Breakfast: 1 serving Mediterranean scramble, coffee with 8 ounces of non-fat milk, 1 slice of 100% whole wheat bread, 1/2 cup of grapes.

Lunch: 1 serving Asian Quinoa Salad (1/2 serving), 1/2 cup baby carrots, 1 medium peach.

Snack: 20 almonds, 1 banana

Dinner: 1 serving of orange chicken and 1 cup of brown rice, 1 cup of steamed spinach, 1 serving of mixed berries.

Day 13

Breakfast: 1 serving English muffin with Berries, 1 hard-boiled egg, and coffee with up to 8 ounces of non-fat milk.

Lunch: 1 serving pomegranate salad with 2 tbsps garlicky balsamic vinaigrette, 1 100% whole wheat pita bread, 1 medium peach.

Snack: ¼ cup hummus dip with baby carrots and sliced bell pepper

Dinner: 1 serving baked sunflower Seed-crusted turkey cutlets, 1 ½ cups roasted mixed vegetables, 1 medium baked sweet potato with 1 tbsp butter, 1 serving fruit Salad.

Day 14

Breakfast: 1 serving morning burrito, 2 slices 100% whole wheat toast with 2 tbsps 100% fruit jam and green tea.

Lunch: 1 serving Greek salad with 1 tbsp lemon vinaigrette, 4 ounces grilled or baked boneless, skinless chicken breast, 1 medium apple, 20 almonds.

Snack: 8 ounces of non-fat plain yogurt and 1 cup mixed berries.

Dinner: 1 serving Thai curried Vegetables, with 3 ounces baked or grilled boneless, skinless chicken breast, 1 cup brown rice, 1 mini banana split.

Day 15

Breakfast: 1 serving garden tuna sandwich, 1 hard-boiled egg, 1 slice 100% whole wheat toast

Lunch: 1 serving turkey fajitas bowl, ¼ cup guacamole, 1 medium orange

Snack: 1 100% whole wheat English muffin with 2 tbsps peanut butter or almond butter and 1 sliced banana.

Dinner: 1 serving pesto Salmon, 1 ½ cups sauteed vegetables, 1 cup orange chicken and brown rice, 1 cup frozen grapes.

Day 16

Breakfast: 1 serving of egg and tomato melts, with 1 cup diced vegetable and 1 cup tropical smoothie.

Lunch: 2 cups dark green salad with 1 tbsp olive oil and lemon dressing, ½ cup chickpeas.

Snack: ½ cup plain Greek yogurt, 4 whole grain crackers.

Dinner: 2 fish tacos, 1 cup pinto beans, ½ cup tropical salsa, 2 slices grilled pineapple.

Day 17

Breakfast: 2 pieces of whole-wheat toast with 1 tbsp of jelly or jam, ½ cup of fresh orange juice, and 1 medium apple.

Lunch: 3 ounces of lean chicken breast with 2 cups of green salad, 1 ½ ounces of low-fat cheese, and 1 cup of brown rice.

Snack: ½ cup of canned peaches and 1 cup of low-fat yogurt.

Dinner: 3 ounces of salmon cooked in 1 tsp of vegetable oil, 1 cup of boiled potatoes, and 1 ½ cups of boiled vegetables.

Day 18

Breakfast: 1 cup of skim milk, 1 cup of oatmeal, ½ cup of raspberries, ½ cup of fresh orange juice.

Lunch: salad made with 4 ½ ounces of grilled tuna, 1 boiled egg, 2 cups of green salad, ½ cup of cherry tomatoes, and 2 tbsps of low-fat dressing.

Snack: ½ cup of canned pears, 1 cup of papaya goodness.

Dinner: 3 ounces of beef brisket, 1 cup of mixed vegetables, 1 cup of brown rice.

Day 19

Breakfast: 1 serving banana almond smoothie, coffee with up to 8 ounces of non-fat milk, 1 slice 100% whole wheat toast with 1 tbsp 100% fruit raspberry jam.

Lunch: 1 serving tuna Salad, with ½ sliced avocado, ½ 100% whole wheat pita bread, and 1 medium orange.

Snack: 1 medium sliced apple, 2 tbsp peanut butter.

Dinner: 1 serving turkey chili with 2 tbsps shredded cheddar cheese, small potato salad, 1 serving berry orange mix.

Day 20

Breakfast: 1 serving veggie frittata with caramelized onions, ½ cup mixed berries, and coffee with up to 8 ounces of non-fat milk.

Lunch: 2 servings chicken pasta salad, 1 cup sliced carrot, bell pepper, and cucumber with 2 tablespoons basic vinaigrette, 1 medium pear.

Snack: 4 ounces of non-fat cottage cheese, ¼ cup raw unsalted cashews, 1 medium sliced apple.

Dinner: 1 serving of beef stroganoff, 1 serving of grilled asparagus, 1 cup of brown rice.

Day 21

Breakfast: 1 serving melon melange smoothie, 1 serving broccoli omelet.

Lunch: 1 serving of fried rice, 3 ounces grilled boneless, skinless chicken breast, 1 cup of grapes

Snack: 1 cup air-popped popcorn, ½ cup baby carrots, ½ sliced medium apple.

Dinner: 1 serving maple roasted tofu, 1 medium mashed sweet potato with 1 tsp butter, 1 serving Greek salad with 1 tbsp lemon vinaigrette, 1 cup mixed berries.

Day 22

Breakfast: 1 serving of banana oatmeal pancake.

Lunch: 1 serving of beef brisket, 1 serving of black-eyed pea salad, 1 medium orange

Snack: 1 cup of fruit salad.

Dinner: 1 serving cauliflower carrot soup, 1 serving Mexican fruit salad, 1 slice grilled pineapple.

Day 23

Breakfast: 1 serving triple breakfast strata, 1 hard-boiled egg, and 1 slice 100% whole wheat toast.

Lunch: 1 serving of corn pudding, 1 cup of roasted vegetables, and 1 apple.

Snack: ½ cup unsalted nuts, 1 apple, and 1 banana.

Dinner: 1 serving of grilled collard greens, and 1 cup of frozen grapes.

Day 24

Breakfast: 1 nutty banana pancake, 8 ounces of non-fat milk, ½ grapefruit.

Lunch: 1 serving Healthy Cobb Salad with 1 tbsp basic vinaigrette, ½ 100% whole wheat pita bread, 1 cup grapes.

Snack: ¼ cup hummus with 1 cup cherry tomatoes, sliced bell pepper, cucumber, 2 tbsp hazelnuts

Dinner: 2 slices Mexican pizza, with 5 ounces grilled or baked boneless, skinless chicken breast, 2 servings Greek salad with 2 tbsp lemon vinaigrette, 1 serving arugula smoothie.

Day 25

Breakfast: 1 cup of peanut butter overnight oatmeal with 1 cup of skim milk, ½ cup of blueberries, and ½ cup of fresh orange juice.

Lunch: chicken salad made with 3 ounces of lean chicken breast, 1 tbsp of mayonnaise, 2 cups of green salad, ½ cup of cherry tomatoes, ½ tbsp of seeds, and 4 whole-grain crackers.

Snack: 1 banana and ½ cup of almonds.

Dinner: 1 serving of quick chili with 1 cup of boiled potatoes, ½ cup of broccoli, and ½ cup (75 grams) of green peas.

Day 26

Breakfast: 1 serving of applesauce, baked oatmeal bars, 1 hard-boiled egg, and 8 ounces of non-fat milk.

Lunch: 1 serving of grilled chicken with black bean salsa, 1 cup baby carrots and sliced bell peppers, 1 cup grapes.

Snack: 8 ounces peach and raspberry parfait, 1 cup mixed berries, 20 almonds.

Dinner: 2 servings roasted butternut squash soup, topped with 1 tbsp low-fat yogurt, 1 serving mixed bean salad, with 2 tbsps dressing, 1 oatmeal Cookie.

Day 27

Breakfast: 1 serving Watermelon Aguas Frescas, 1/2 100% whole wheat English muffin with 2 tbsps peanut butter, coffee with up to 8 ounces of non-fat milk.

Lunch: ½ cup black beans with 2 corn tortillas and 2 tbsps cheddar cheese, 1/4 cup salsa, ½ sliced avocado, small spinach salad with 1 cup diced bell pepper, cucumber, and grape tomatoes, 2 tbsps basic vinaigrette.

Snack: 20 hazelnuts, 1 serving orange strawberry twirl, ½ cup sliced strawberries

Dinner: 1 serving brown rice risotto with lamb, 1 serving brussels sprouts casserole, 1 medium baked sweet potato, 1 serving island chiller.

Day 28

Breakfast: ½ cup instant oatmeal, 1 mini whole wheat bagel, 1 tbsp peanut butter, 1 medium banana, 1 cup low-fat milk.

Lunch: 1 serving of chicken breast sandwich, 1 serving of potato salad, 1 cup of cookies, and a cream shake.

Snacks: ½ cup unsalted almonds, ¼ cup raisins, 1 cup fat-free fruit yogurt.

Dinner: 1 serving grilled Asian salmon, 1 ½ cups sauteed vegetables, 1 cup cilantro-lime brown rice, 1 cup frozen grapes.

Day 29

Breakfast: ¾ cup bran flakes cereal, 1 slice whole wheat bread, 1 tsp margarine, 1 cup fresh orange juice.

Lunch: beef barbecue sandwich, 1 cup Mexican summer salad, 1 medium orange.

Snacks: 1 100% whole wheat English muffin with 2 tbsps peanut butter or almond butter and 1 sliced banana.

Dinner: 3-ounce cod, 1 ½ cups brown rice, 1 cup spinach, cooked from frozen, sauteed with 1 tsp canola oil, 1 tbsp almonds, 1 small cornbread muffin topped with 1 tsp soft margarine.

Day 30

Breakfast: 1 slice whole wheat bread, 1 cup fruit yogurt, 1 medium peach, ½ cup grape juice.

Lunch: 1 serving shrimp kebab, ½ cup guacamole, with 1 cup baby carrots, 1 medium orange (small).

Snack: ⅓ cup almonds, unsalted 0 1 cup apple juice 21 ¼ cup apricots 3 1 cup low-fat milk

Dinner: 1 serving of steamy salmon chowder, 1 serving of grilled asparagus, 1 cup brown rice, 1 cup melon, and orange slushy.

Measurement Conversion

Measure	Equivalent	Metric
1 teaspoon	⅓ tablespoon	5 millimeters
1 tablespoon	3 teaspoons	14.8 millimeters
¼ cup	4 tablespoons	59.16 millimeters
½ cup	8 tablespoons	118.3 millimeters
1 cup	16 tablespoons	236.8 millimeters
1 pint	2 cups or 16 fluid ounces	473.6 millimeters
1 quart	4 cups or 32 fluid ounces	947.2 millimeters
I liter	4 cups + 3 ½ tablespoons	1000 millimeters
1 ounce (dry)	2 tablespoons	28.35 grams
1 pound	16 ounces	453.49 grams
2.21 pounds	35.3 ounces	1 kilogram

Conclusion

Hypertension is the leading cause of death in the United States today. Approximately 50% of adults suffering from unregulated hypertension possess a blood pressure level equal to 140/90 mmHg or higher. Unfortunately, this disease puts this spectrum at higher risk of heart disease, kidney failure, stroke, and many deadly outcomes.

Several factors could increase the risk of diseases, from stroke, heart failure, diabetes, cancer, and beyond. They include

- Age
- Poor diet
- Being overweight or obese
- Family history/genes
- High blood pressure or cholesterol
- History of smoking
- Excessive alcohol use
- Staying inactive
- Irregular blood sugar levels.

While medications can treat and reduce high blood pressure, changing your lifestyle can also help control and manage high blood pressure and improve your overall health. For example, you can try the following:

- Eat a heart-healthy diet with less salt
- Get regular physical activity
- Maintain a healthy weight
- Limit alcohol
- Not smoking
- Getting 7 to 9 hours of sleep daily.

Thankfully, this is what the DASH diet is about. Dietary Approaches to Stop Hypertension are a blessing that keeps on giving. This approach was specifically designed to treat and reduce high blood pressure in hypertensive patients. Many groups, including the Mayo Clinic and American Heart Association, endorse the DASH Diet.

As already discussed, eating a healthful diet and staying active could reduce your risk of breast cancer, heart disease, and osteoporosis. The DASH diet offers numerous health benefits and can help with weight loss while increasing your body's metabolic rate.

Dash diet has become a staple for people with high blood pressure and other heart-related conditions. So many people can now embark on a new wellness path to keep their bodies strong and functioning optimally. The best part about following this diet is that it allows you to create a customizable, balanced eating plan without using unique or hard-to-find ingredients.

You don't need to starve or deny yourself the pleasure of tasty meals. Instead, the DASH diet encourages you to eat healthy quality meals against the quantity. Every essential vitamin and component for the body's healthy functioning is included in the DASH diet. This contains various vitamins, calcium, proteins, fiber, and other valuable nutrients.

My core purpose of this fully comprehensive **DASH Diet Cookbook for Beginners 2023** is to help people achieve optimal health and wellness. This book contains simple recipes with everyday ingredients to help you adapt to the plan.

I have shared 190 DASH diet recipes for every meal, including hearty breakfasts and satisfying dinners. It also contains tips for navigating the grocery store and choosing the right DASH diet foods for you and your family.

These recipes focus on lowering your blood pressure, weight loss, and improving your lifestyle in general. Now that you've discovered amazing DASH diet recipes, it's time to put what you've learned into practice. Get to your kitchen and start cooking.

Finally, if you enjoyed this book, please be kind enough to leave a review for this book on Amazon. Your efforts will be greatly appreciated!

Click here to leave a review for this book on Amazon!

Thank you, and good luck on your healthy path.

Indeks

So What Food Is Off-Limit?

Compared to other popular diets, there is a shorter list of rules you must follow on the DASH diet. However, when following the DASH plan, there are certain foods you should leave out of your grocery list and avoid consuming. Unfortunately, you may find some of your favorite foods on the *not to eat* list.

The DASH diet limits foods that negatively impact your blood pressure and heart health. Some of these foods are;

High sodium foods

By drastically cutting down on high-sodium foods, you decrease the risk of hypertension, stroke, and other heart diseases. So avoid these items:

- Table salt
- Fast food
- Pre-packaged food
- Processed meats (red meat, deli meat)
- Packaged snacks high in fat, salt, and sugar
- White rice
- Enriched pasta

Saturated Fats

It would help if you reduced your intake of food high in saturated fats. For example,

- Cream
- Butter
- Whole-fat milk
- Pastries
- Whole-fat cheese
- Fatty cuts of meat
- Poultry with skin
- Lard
- Deep-fried foods

Added Sugar

Foods with added sugar, such as cakes, cookies, or sugar-sweetened beverages like iced tea, sodas, or fruit juice, are highly discouraged on the DASH diet. To avoid falling back on your diet, I encourage you to get used to reading ingredient labels on packaged foods.

Most packed foods have Nutritional Facts labels that help you decide how they fit into your DASH diet.

Alcohol

Staying hydrated while adjusting to the DASH diet may help you to maintain your energy levels and stay full between meals. Drink lots of water to quench your thirst; there is no room for alcoholic beverages with this plan.

Alcohol contains calories that do not comply with your DASH diet and can damage your body's vital organs.

In conclusion, the DASH diet is not a starvation diet. Instead, it is designed to make you eat regularly and eat food that keeps you satisfied. By following this plan, you will not suffer fatigue or exhaustion. But like other healthy diets, incorporating physical activity will amplify the improvements you see in your body and health.

Part 3

Following Dash Diet

Here, you will find healthy tips and tricks on following the DASH diet and answers to your FAQs about this eating plan.

Chapter 8: Best Dash diet Tips and Tricks

The DASH diet is a lifelong approach to healthy eating, so you must be prepared for a lifestyle change. However, not everyone adapts well to change, and it is understandable. Transitioning to the DASH diet plan can be challenging for some, especially beginners.

Thankfully, in this chapter, I have shared many helpful tips and tricks to help you navigate this process and grocery shopping tips to help you get started.

DASH Diet Tips

- **Don't try to change everything at once:** The DASH diet is not a quick fix; it's best to begin gradually to build your way up. With this diet plan, gradual change is more sustainable and rewarding.

- **Your meals don't have to be boring**: Instead, make your plate colorful by adding fruits or vegetables to every meal. Add 5 servings of fruits and vegetables per day.

- **Limit salt when cooking:** Instead, consider seasoning with condiments the same way you would with salt. For example, use aromatic vegetables like garlic, onions or peppers, herbs, spices, or with fruits.

- **Stay hydrated:** Drink a lot of water daily and with each meal. Avoid alcohol, sodas, or sugary beverages.

- **Rethink your snacking options:** Go for unsalted food products with no added salt or lower sodium substitutes for your favorite snacks.

- **Plan your meals around seasonal fruits and vegetables**: To get the highest nutrients, buy foods that are in season. Also, keep fresh-cut fruits handy to replace sugary treats for healthy convenience.

- **Boost flavors naturally:** To boost flavors without adding fats or extra salt, roast your vegetables to intensify their tastes, or use fresh herbs and ground spices.

- **Watch portion and serving sizes:** Pay attention to the amount of food you are consuming. So understand your portions and serving sizes. Keep a measuring cup handy when preparing your meals and snacks.

- **Get a food journal:** This will help you track what you eat and the days you defaulted.

- **Get physically active:** Exercise is integral to a healthy lifestyle. Rather than staying sedentary, aim for at least 2 hours and 30 min of exercise to combine with your DASH diet.

DASH Diet Shopping Tips

Large displays, bargain prices, coupon offers, and promos may draw your attention while you are in the grocery store. Follow these shopping tips to help you stay focused on your DASH diet goals:

- **Before shopping, make a list:** Look through this cookbook, decide on your meal for the week, and write down the ingredients. This list makes you less likely to be tempted by unhealthy foods.
- **Eat first:** Do not shop for groceries when you're hungry. If you shop when you're hungry, everything on the shelf looks appealing, which makes it hard to resist those high-fat, high-sodium items.
- **Read nutritional labels:** It is important to read the nutritional labels of items you want to buy. Most packaged foods in the U.S. have a Nutrition Facts label to help you decide how they fit into your plan. Watch out for added sugar like glucose, high fructose corn syrup, sucrose, reduced sodium, and fat products. Compare like items and choose the beneficial one.
- **Buy fresh items instead of processed foods:** For healthier choices, fresh foods contain less sodium, added fat, and sugar than their packaged counterparts. Plus, they have more health-promoting vitamins, minerals, and fiber than processed foods.
- **Avoid the middle aisles:** One way to avoid being tricked into buying processed foods is to avoid the center aisles of a grocery store. It is because most processed and packed foods are sold there. Your attention should be on the outer aisles, where you'll find whole foods, fresh produce, low-fat dairy products, and lean meats. Or better still, shop at the local farmer's market to get great nutritional value.
- **Stock up on DASH staples:** If you have more healthy foods in your kitchen, you will likely prepare healthy dishes. You should phase out processed, packaged foods, junk, preseasoned sauces, etc., and stock up on healthy items, so they are readily available.

Tricks for Cooking

Unhealthy cooking habits can sabotage your other efforts to stick to the DASH diet. Use these tips to help reduce sodium and fat:

- Serve lean meat without heavy sauces. Try to consume three to six servings of lean poultry daily.
- Again, enhance flavor without adding salt or fat using herbs, spices, flavored vinegar, onions, peppers, ginger, lemon, garlic or garlic powder, or sodium-free bouillon.
- Replace full-fat dairy with reduced-fat or fat-free versions. If you find it difficult to digest milk products, you can buy lactose-free milk or opt for lactase-enzyme pills with milk products. They are available at drug stores.
- Many canned foods contain high sodium levels, making them saltier than fresh ones. Asides from tomatoes, I recommend you give your canned foods, such as beans and vegetables, a good rinse before using them to wash away some excess salt.
- Finally, if you take medications to control your high blood pressure, do not skip them. However, inform your doctor that you are now eating the DASH way.